A JOHN CATT PUBLICATION

NEIL & JANE HAWKES

THE INNER CURRICULUM

How to nourish wellbeing, resilience and self-leadership

The new era in education...

First Published 2018

by John Catt Educational Ltd,
15 Riduna Park, Station Road,
Melton, Woodbridge IP12 1QT

Tel: +44 (0) 1394 389850
Email: enquiries@johncatt.com
Website: www.johncatt.com

ISBN: 978 1 911382 65 2

Set and designed by John Catt Educational Limited

We would like to dedicate this book to all those who give hope to humanity through what we describe as Values-based Living (VbL). As you have chosen to work with this guide you must be one of them. Our hope is that our proposed Inner Curriculum will support you in your efforts to nurture wellbeing, resilience and self-leadership, thereby enabling humanity to flourish and our world to be sustainable.

Praise for
The Inner Curriculum

Neil Hawkes' Values-based Education (VbE) has been highly successful in helping schools in England and worldwide become more compassionate, character-building places. With this new book, he and his wife Jane are expanding their reach by offering a practical guide to the inner changes needed to support VbE. I believe this work has the power to transform education in the direction needed to address the massive problems our planet is facing by helping children become not only more self-aware, but also committed to positive change.

Richard C. Schwartz, PhD
Developer of the Internal Family Systems model of psychotherapy
Faculty, Department of Psychiatry, Harvard University Medical School

This charismatic book shows how every teacher can contribute to a better world, where the desire to love outweighs the instinct to fear and dislike.

Lord Richard Layard

This book contains the formula for changing the world. There is no doubt in my mind that values-based education is the key to creating a compassionate, peaceful future for humanity.

Richard Barrett, Director of the Academy for the Advancement of Human Values

Neil and Jane Hawkes work in Values-based Education has influenced education all over the world. I can testify to the effects it had on Australian education during the time of the Australian Values Education Program (2003-2010), a federally-funded innovation in values-based learning and teaching. Their work on the Inner Curriculum continues their important work in demonstrating that the choices before us are not in the form of 'wellbeing versus results' but rather 'results through wellbeing'. Increasingly, neuroscience is providing insights that conform to the Hawkes thesis that the learning brain is most active and engaged when our emotions, thoughts and feelings are in alignment, and when values of empathy, altruism, generosity and justice are instilled and determining the nature of the learning environment.

Terry Lovat
Emeritus Professor, University of Newcastle, Australia
Honorary Research Fellow, University of Oxford, UK

Neil and Jane Hawkes have already transformed education with their Values-based Education approach to nurturing effective inter-personal relationships. This book introduces the world to a new generation of VbE, the Inner Curriculum. It is a whole new approach to education that empowers schools to address some of the challenges to our children's mental dispositions laid by modern society.

This is a book that every teacher in the world should read, because it will help them transform their teaching from simple conveying of information into developing the capability of every one of their students to realise their full potential. Exciting stuff!

Nigel Cohen
Strategic Director of VbE and CEO of the Inclusivity Trust

As part of our staff induction everyone at Aureus School read Neil's book *From My Heart*. I have since met Neil and Jane in person. They are everything I knew they would be! I was excited to read the *The Inner Curriculum* to extend my previous thinking and learning. Passionate about wellbeing and resilience for our staff and for our students, the focus on nurturing the authentic self and developing human consciousness is what is missing from our high stakes system and exams driven curriculum. Neil and Jane's unwavering commitment to the whole child entitlement is refreshing and their exploration of the place for the human condition is fascinating. I am with them, that we need to put the soul back into our schools!

Hannah Wilson
Executive Headteacher at Aureus School and Aureus Primary School

The most exquisite flowers need the right conditions to flourish. Neil and Jane Hawkes in their superb book on the Inner Curriculum articulate the values and the pre-conditions that enable children to grow into beautiful people.

Andrew Fuller
Clinical Psychologist, author and Family Therapist, Australia

The Inner Curriculum is essential reading for anybody who has any involvement in school leadership. Values-based Education and the Inner Curriculum are key components for ensuring you have a happy, healthy and positive school, where all children achieve their very best. Neil and Jane are the leading experts in this field and have ensured this book is easy to understand and applicable to all schools.

Tim Handley
Teacher, Norwich, UK

Education should be about developing the whole child: helping them to achieve great academic outcomes and shaping their character so that they are able to make the best use of experiences and opportunities. Neil and Jane's influence has reminded us at Stamford Welland Academy that teachers and school leaders are the frontline in ensuring that our work on developing values and character in our children is our core business and not a distraction from it. Their work challenges us all to think again about what is education and what is it for.

Anthony Partington
Executive Principal, Stamford Welland Academy
Executive Director of Education, CMAT

This book is an innovative and powerful approach to understanding how having a strong mind and spirit aligned with powerful values is essential in developing our character to become a whole person. The inner curriculum is a powerful tool not only for children but for adults too. It helps us to have wisdom to change the world for the better.

Floyd Woodrow MBE DCM

Neil and Jane's book is essential reading for all in schools. Values-based Education and its Inner Curriculum is a unique and effective approach to teaching positive communication. My fellow early years teachers and I at Alfaheidi preschool in Iceland encourage teachers and parents around the world to join us.

Rakel Yr Isaksen
Special needs coordinator and early years teacher at Alfaheidi preschool in Iceland

In this thought-provoking book from one of the foremost authorities on character education, Dr Neil Hawkes makes yet another major contribution to the Values-based Education movement. Whether you are a parent, educator, policy maker or concerned citizen, this book gives the reader an honest and heartfelt account of the problems facing schools today, but most importantly the reasons to be optimistic about the future. Neil and Jane's vision of an 'Inner Curriculum' attest to the power of character we all have within ourselves to ensure that every child can fulfil their potential. Hopeful and daring, *The Inner Curriculum* will challenge school leaders to reflect on the cultural beliefs, thoughts, actions and habits driving their organisation and how best to positively shape the character to truly open the minds of the new generation.

Dr Andrew Reay, author of the *Power of Character: Lessons from the frontline* & co-founder of a values-driven Multi-Academy Trust

The Inner Curriculum will be essential reading for all people who value the importance of childhood, and who are in a position to shape future lives; that's all of us, I think! Neil and Jane Hawkes visionary thinking and work has already had a massively positive impact on the lives of the children, staff, parents and governors at College Road Primary School... and there's more to come!

Jim Wallace
Headteacher, College Road School

As a class teacher I have found that values-based education ensures all pupils develop holistically. The principles of the inner curriculum explored in this book build on this. I know applying a cosmic-centric approach to learning will continue to improve the wellbeing and resilience of the young people we work with, transforming their education and their lives.

Katie Greenwood, Values Leader
Sandylands School, Morecambe

This inspiring book is one of the very few in the general area of personal, moral and social education which both is philosophically sound and yet draws upon a rich account of life in classrooms. That is reflected in success, which VbE has had in schools worldwide – an incredible achievement. It challenges the dominance of the performance measures that now too often shape educational practice.

Professor Richard Pring, Former Director, Education Department, Oxford University

Education is not just about filling up a vase but lighting a flame. In The Inner Curriculum, Neil and Jane Hawkes persuasively show how this flame can be fuelled by compassion, honesty, tolerance and other fundamental human values that allow young human beings to flourish and become of service to the world.

Matthieu Ricard, author of *Happiness: A Guide to Developing Life's Most Important Skill*

Acknowledgements

This book and guide exists because of the generous support of many people who have spoken with us and influenced our thinking. As there are so many of you, it would be wrong to name a few, but you know who you are. To each one of you, we say a heartfelt thank you for your generosity of spirit.

We have been privileged to visit many wonderful schools in various parts of the world that are working tirelessly to bring quality education to their pupils – often in challenging circumstances. The staff, pupils, parents and other stakeholders in these schools have been so generous in helping us form our views that we share in this book – again, thank you.

Lastly, thank you to the intellectual giants of the world of education, psychotherapy and interpersonal neurobiology on whose shoulders we sit. It is your thinking which has inspired us – a huge thank you.

Contents

Foreword

The context, challenge and a solution...

We have written this transformational guide for developing wellbeing, resilience and self-leadership, because we passionately believe that the greatest resource that humanity has is its children: our future prosperity as a species rests with them. Our experience reminds us that it is the quality of parenting, health, care and education that are the main determinants for living a life that gives children a chance to achieve wellbeing; developing in them character traits that contribute to the wellbeing of others and our world.

The process of life creates physical and psychological challenges that none escape. Each epoch has brought with it particular benefits but also challenges, whether this is war, famine or disease. Our present time has brought high population growth, an existential challenge to the Earth's resources, breakdown of traditional family and social structures, a technological revolution, rapid communication, high mobility, challenges to social norms and the political status quo, to name but a few.

Within this context most countries continue promoting an industrial model of education based mainly on structures introduced in the 19th century. Reforms since then have merely added to or tinkered with the established education system. Today, the role of teachers has never been so complex and the expectations on them and their schools have never been higher.

We think that there is an urgent need for national and international debates about what constitutes a good education in the context of life in the 21st century. These debates should be research driven rather than centred on a country's political whims, or any other form of bias based on ideology or institutional power.

We are fortunate to work with many talented teachers and school leaders in a number of countries who, despite the limitations of their educational system, create outstanding learning and teaching environments that both nurture and educate children holistically. They ensure that pupils are given opportunities to develop all aspects of their multi intelligences and do not limit them to the linguistic and mathematical domains of learning. They achieve amazing results, empowering pupils to achieve excellence academically and build positive character traits too. These educators we describe as heroes, who are leading the drive for a transformation of the system that will give their pupils an education that nurtures wellbeing and resilience.

We are driven to write this guide because we think that universally teachers, and support staff, need to be given the help that comes from knowledge, both of their own internal world and how to help children and young people understand theirs. The result being a profound change in self and other awareness that forms a well educated, compassionate self-led human being. Therefore, we call for a reappraisal of the role of the teacher, which we argue should include a pedagogy built on self-knowledge.

We hope this guide will also support parents, young adults, psychotherapists, social workers, community leaders, teacher educators and others who want to help children, young people and themselves to flourish.

It is our hope too that our notion of the Inner Curriculum, as an initial guide for Values-based Living (VbL), will be seriously considered and applied universally by educational, social and political leaders as a model for transforming education that will enhance it for the benefit both of the individual and society in general.

An Introduction to Inspire You

Welcome to our book about the Inner Curriculum, which is a guide about how to develop wellbeing, resilience and self-leadership in children and you. Thank you for choosing to read and – we hope – use this guide. We are confident that you will be inspired by it and empowered to apply our practical ideas. We hope that you will agree that the powerful quotes that follow underline the urgency for developing wellbeing, resilience and self-leadership.

Dr. Sarah Wollaston, chair of the UK's House of Commons Health Committee remarked:

'With half of all mental illness starting before the age of 15, and three-quarters by aged 18, the government and educators must ensure sufficient time is allowed for activities in schools and colleges that develop the lifelong skills children and young people need to support their wellbeing.'

Dr. Dan Siegel, Neurobiologist reminds us that good interpersonal relationships are paramount in the classroom: 'In many ways the relationship between student and teacher parallels the attachment between child and parent.'

We, Neil and Jane Hawkes, believe that self-leadership, wellbeing and resilience can be nurtured:

'Our experience of working with schools in many countries has convinced us that it is through an understanding about how our internal world shapes our lives that we can transform our sense of self-leadership, wellbeing, our relationships, resilience, social structures and systems – including schooling.'

It is our experience that without high levels of wellbeing and resilience, pupils are unable to function well, build strong and positive relationships, or get the most out of their education. VbE has recognised this for many years; our work has been to support schools in creating authentic values-based cultures, which promote wellbeing and resilience for all.

We have been mindful to create this book as a guide; one that gives you both an understanding of the transformational theoretical ideas underpinning it and a range of practical exercises that will support its implementation. Hence why we have written this book in two main parts, followed by a postscript. After this introduction, the two parts, each with its own chapters, may be considered as two books but we would highly recommend that you read Part A before delving into the practicalities and applications inherent in Part B. The book ends with a postscript.

Part A. In this theoretical part, we give you an overview of Values-based Education (VbE): the Inner Curriculum (IC) and their relationship with each other. We aim to inspire you so that you will want to adopt or further develop VbE and IC in your school, classroom and home.

Part B. How to implement the Inner Curriculum.

This practical guide will give you lots of ideas that will help you to develop wellbeing, resilience and self-leadership in children and you.

As we began working on this book we asked ourselves why does wellbeing have a number of different spellings? Interestingly, it is a concept that has no agreed spelling and you will see it written as well being, well-being or wellbeing. In this guide, to be consistent, we use the spelling wellbeing.

The next question we pondered was, what is wellbeing? The term has been in general use for some time and academics argue over its definition; in fact, many definitions are really descriptions of wellbeing rather than definitions. Dictionaries generally give the definition as, 'the state of being comfortable, healthy, or happy'. This may be traced back to Aristotle's notion of Eudemonia, human flourishing. Our understanding is that wellbeing can be defined in two ways: firstly, as a background state of mind that each of us feels generally about our life; secondly, a more transient, fluctuating state of mind that depends on the availability of a range of psychological, social and physical resources we need to meet life's challenges. The availability of these resources leads to the development of resilience, which is the process of adapting well and 'bouncing back' in the face of adversity, trauma, tragedy, threats or significant sources of stress. Resilience is not a trait you have or don't have. It involves thoughts and behaviours that can be learned and developed in all of us.

To illustrate what we mean by wellbeing, may we invite you to consider two questions?

1. On a scale of 1-10, with 10 being the highest score, what intuitively is your general wellbeing quotient?

2. Next, on the same scale, consider a time when your wellbeing quotient felt much lower? Perhaps you were being challenged by an event or situation that affected your sense of wellbeing?

We hope that taking time to consider these questions has helped you to understand the difference between our general feeling of wellbeing and how we may feel almost moment-to-moment. If you gave yourself a low score in answer to the first question then we hope that by reading this guide it will help you to have a greater sense of wellbeing.

If your score for the second question is low, but your answer for the first was fairly high, then you will find that it will be the degree of resilience that you have acquired through life's experiences that will allow you to bounce back to your 'normal' quotient.

We hope that by reflecting on your own wellbeing, you will see why it is so important to help children to develop the ability to be resilient in the face of life's inevitable challenges. We have written this guide to help you and any children or pupils who you are supporting, whether at home or in school, to develop resilience and a greater sense of wellbeing. To support you, we have coined an expression, the Inner Curriculum, to use as an umbrella term for describing the key elements that promote wellbeing, resilience and self-leadership.

We believe that the Inner Curriculum is where the profound insights of education, psychotherapy, interpersonal neurobiology and the wisdom of humanity converge, thereby enhancing a child's innate capacity to experience wellbeing and resilience, love learning and develop altruistic behaviour. Implementing the Inner Curriculum takes each of us on a unique journey to release our true essence, distinctive genius, and our infinite potential.

For teachers the term curriculum is a familiar one, meaning all that they intend to do in school to enable a child to be a successful learner. The curriculum is made up of knowledge to learn, skills to experience and dispositions to be acquired. We believe that such a curriculum only partially and inadequately satisfies the complex range of personal and social needs of young people living in the 21st century. There remains, we believe, an existential vacuum, which we think can be filled by an understanding and mastery of our internal worlds, hence the Inner Curriculum.

The Inner Curriculum is one of the core elements and a natural outcome of a powerful cultural enhancement tool called Values-based Education. VbE is recognised by educators as a holistic process for character education, one that builds on the innate qualities of people. It is a potent force for positive transformational change in schools and educational systems.

In her book, *Taught Not Caught: Educating for 21st Century Character*, Nicky Morgan, former Secretary of State for Education in the UK, reminds us of the need to balance the knowledge and character-based curriculum and refers to the processes involved in VbE. She writes:

'The English education system is only doing half the job it needs to prepare our children for the 21st century… employers are putting an even greater premium on character traits such as resilience, persistence, grit, leadership, self-awareness and self-efficacy…

'For the individual, developing positive character traits gives them improved self-control, confidence and behaviour, which is expected to lead to better academic outcomes, improved employment outcomes and a better quality of life as well as a sense of personal flourishing.

'In his book, *From My Heart: Transforming Lives Through Values*, Dr. Neil Hawkes writes... The whole school community (staff, pupils, parents and community representatives) is involved in understanding, identifying and shaping the values education policy...'

Research supports Nicky's view that VbE encourages the development of positive personal and pro-social character traits and has a profound impact on school culture.

Anthony Partington, the Principal of Stamford Welland Academy, Executive Director of Education, CMAT, endorses the impact of VbE in his secondary school:

'Our trust of schools was founded on values that Henry Morris, the great pioneer of secondary schooling in Cambridgeshire, put in place: every child should be known, supported and valued through lifelong learning. We further believe that if you value your people, greatness will follow.

'Working to develop a Values-based Education at Stamford Welland Academy, whose predecessor school had lost the trust of the community, with Neil and Jane's inspiration has ensured rapid improvements. We have been able to articulate the 'why' of improvement, as well as the 'what' and the 'how'.

'As well as retaining and developing our students and staff, these clear values that we live out in the academic and parallel curriculum opportunities and experiences have encouraged more to join us, to adopt and maintain lifelong values for learning and restored the community's trust in the school.'

Primary VbE schools, such as Sandylands in Morecambe, receive outstanding reports from inspectors for their development of behaviour and personal/social development:

'The school offers an excellent personal, social, health and citizenship curriculum that is woven into an award-winning, values-based curriculum. All pupils work towards a 'values baccalaureate'. Completing activities and evidencing skills related to values such as thoughtfulness, resilience and cooperation can achieve this. Pupils who are responsible for championing values work with adults to devise projects and activities to support pupils to succeed.

'The high profile given to developing pupils' life skills promotes the value and importance of being healthy, responsible and well-balanced citizens. This, coupled with pupils' increasing aspirations and awareness of global issues and events, immerses pupils in finding out about themselves and others. As a result, pupils are developing as empathetic, thoughtful and compassionate citizens.'

Why do VbE schools have this impact? VbE's main focus is on explicitly learning about, experiencing and living an ethical vocabulary based on positive, universal human values such as respect, honesty, tolerance and compassion. By living these values – principles that guide thinking and behaviour – habitually they become a person's virtues (inherent qualities). Pupils in VbE schools learn about values experientially and are expected to demonstrate the values in their behaviour, which create a positive climate for learning. The outcome is that young people develop greater conscious awareness that forms their ethical and emotional intelligence. VbE is described by teachers as enhancing mental wellbeing, altruistic behaviour, academic diligence and an empathic awareness of the interconnectedness of people and the natural world encouraging Values-based Living (VbL).

We are often asked what the outcome of being a VbE school is? Why are they so very important and what impact do they have? One consequence, which for us was initially unintended, is that there appears to be a clear economic reason for developing VbE. This is because by deliberately creating a calm and purposeful atmosphere VbE schools create the conditions for children to gain the most from their education and thrive academically.

Emma Trafford, a pupil at West Kidlington during Neil's Headship, wrote to us explaining what the impact had been for her of being educated in a VbE school:

'I think that having a Values-based Education during my time at West Kidlington School had an extremely positive impact on my life, both at the time and even now. I have strong memories of my primary school experience, including reflection times, positive relationships with my classmates and teachers, impactful assemblies and our life-enhancing values. One of my teachers in primary school was the person who inspired me to become a teacher myself. I have recently started my fifth year as a primary school teacher and I am finding myself implementing all the things I learned as a child in my own classroom: ensuring there are reflection times for the children and providing opportunities for deeper thinking around positive human values and global issues. Additionally, I don't think that it is a coincidence that I am still very good friends with many people with whom I went to school and that three out of eight of us are teachers!'

Not only pupils gain from the positive healing and nurturing impact of VbE schools; teachers and support staff are also likely to experience the effects of what we refer to as 'self-energy', a concept that we will explain later. The benefits of VbE for adults include: having higher morale, enjoying their teaching and not feeling the effects of burn out by becoming ill; in extremis having a breakdown and leaving the profession.

VbE create the conditions that lead to profound economic change. Our current economic systems encourage and reward materialism and self-interest. Values-based Living nurtures an alternative consciousness that is focused around mutual cooperation and harmonious coexistence. These are the conditions for peaceful, thriving societies, which we see experienced in communities who fully embrace these ideas. We therefore think that creating a calm and purposeful atmosphere, whether in school, the home or at work should become a core principle for establishing Values-based Living.

Within such a supportive and nurturing atmosphere (ethos) are developed the principles behind the leadership, management, culture and routines of a VbE school that create an environment, which aims to release the creative, enriching dynamic of all members of the school. For instance, a VbE school avoids having hierarchies of relationships only of roles, so everyone is aware that they have different roles but that all are deemed equal as human beings. There is a natural feeling of belonging, teamwork and shared responsibility. Louis Cozolino, in his book, *The Social Neuroscience of Education*, refers to research that shows that the more schools resemble a bureaucratic hierarchy, with rigid authority structures and undemocratic policies, the greater is the likelihood of teacher burnout. Too much emphasis on high stakes testing also creates the conditions for burnout. This research has important consequences for teacher education and a rethink of the educational system *per se*.

We are aware that VbE schools also develop what is called social capital, which means that as cooperative social networks are established, transactions between members of staff are marked by reciprocity, trust and that everyone works for the common good. We are convinced that schools and educational systems urgently need to transform themselves to be more relevant for the challenges, complexities and opportunities of the 21st century. We are confident that they will be helped to do this if they adopt the principles and practices that we propose in this guide.

We live at a time, filled with personal, social and political unrest, which demands that we creatively transform pedagogy, ideas and practices so that education is relevant to the demands of our times. We propose that all children need to understand what it means to be a complete human being; that our future depends on their ability to be humane and in relationship with the natural world. We do not live in the 19th century, but so much of schooling reflects the tradition and mores of that epoch. We think that the greatest inhibitor for positive change is that adults have all been to school. Subsequently, the natural human tendency to mirror and reproduce what we have experienced limits the capacity for meaningful change.

We have a duty to support all young people, who deserve a future full of opportunity that brings personal and social wellbeing – free from the materialistic myths of society. The educational status quo does much to limit the potential of young people, condemning millions to unfulfilled lives, because they are not being given the insights that will help them to find meaning and purpose in their lives and the processes to determine their future happiness.

One of our heroes is Victor Frankl. Neil's reading of Frankl's book, *Man's Search for Meaning*, inspired him and he usually refers to the importance of having a meaning and purpose in your life when he talks about the basics of VbE. He also respects the thoughts of Johann Wolfgang von Goethe. Frankl referred to this philosopher when he was talking to a group of students about what his flying instructor had said to him when he was being given flying lessons.

The instructor had told Frankl that if he were flying to an airport and that there was a crosswind, making his plane fly off course, and then he would have to adjust the plane's height, course and speed to ensure that he reached the destination. Frankl used his experience to quote Goethe, suggesting that his flying lesson was a metaphor for us. 'If you take man as he is you make him worse, but if you take him as he could be then you make him capable of becoming what he could be.' We believe the metaphor holds firm for how we should treat children both at home and in the classroom in order to take the lid off their potential. Such profound thoughts form our beliefs about children and education that create our mission as educators. For us:

'If you treat a child as she is, she will remain how she is. But if you treat her as if she were what she ought to be and could be, she will become what she ought to be and could be.' (Please read she as he too).

We saw this transforming philosophy in practice when we visited King's Leadership Academy in Warrington. No 'glass ceilings' are placed on any student where the Academy's mission is to develop values-driven leaders of the future. Dr. Andrew Reay, Deputy Principal, explains:

'If the whole purpose of a school is to develop every facet of a child, why, then, up and down the country, do the overwhelming majority of our state schools continue to focus far too heavily on the metric of exam results and obsess over Ofsted inspections? What could a paradigm shift in the way we run our schools and classrooms look like and how could it be achieved? Values-based Education, then, is our own paradigm shift.

We at the Great Schools Trust hold the unwavering belief that every child – regardless of background, post-code or starting point – can succeed academically and personally.

'Doing the right thing, being values-based requires a long-term commitment on the part of schools. If we want a fairer, more just, more productive society, we now need to focus more on what Dr. Martin Luther King called the 'content of our character'. People, such as Dr. Hawkes, who are transforming education today, are doing it by building consensus around a common set of guiding principles. There are no shortcuts to good character. It must be grown from the root up and the only way to consistently apply Values-based Education in our schools is to intentionally build students character over the course of time – to be a constant gardener – to engrave a mark on their lives and those of others so deep, that its leaves an enduring imprint.'

In contrast, an outmoded notion of what national and personal success looks like, limits the capacity of pupils to take the lid of their potential. Misguided political systems, such as a heavy-handed inspection system, over-testing of pupils, combined with a lack of understanding about the powerful role of social class, power and money limits the current education system. This produces erroneous outcomes in terms of attitudes, skills and knowledge, which are rendered meaningless when considered against what society actually needs to be harmonious and successful. Currently many education systems condemn many children to a narrow curriculum that limits their intellectual, spiritual, creative and entrepreneurial potential. In contrast, we see VbE in schools such as King's Leadership Academy, as equipping the next generation with the personal and collective wisdom, resourcefulness and resilience needed to meet the challenges that the current unsustainable system create.

We hope though to inspire you to co-create creative learning opportunities for young people by joining our quiet revolution; a revolution of the heart, one that will empower all children to be free from the limitations of social class, patronage, money, power or privilege. Such limiting social factors can be minimised when young people are given the understanding about their own natural innate internal energy, their essence, which we call self-energy. This is an unselfish power, which recognises an interconnected worldview. We believe that this is the energy that is patently manifest in people such as Dr. Martin Luther King Jr., Gandhi and Einstein. It is an energy that challenges the selfish aspects of our nature and therefore can find opposition from people who are dominated by selfish and self-serving aspects of their personalities. Information about the concept of self-energy is not generally available in schools, where the emphasis is on an external curriculum and a worldview that emphasises separateness. We fervently hope that this book will address this serious omission.

The releasing of the power of self-energy is contained in what we have called the Inner Curriculum. We hope that you will enjoy learning about and experiencing aspects of the Inner Curriculum; feeling empowered to use it with yourself, family and pupils at school and in other settings. As a result, we hope you will share with us your experience of working with the Inner Curriculum, so that we can add many more examples of successful practice to this guide in the future.

Now let's delve into Part A…

Part A:

An Overview of Values-based Education and the Inner Curriculum

Chapter 1:
What is Values-based Education?

'Intelligence plus character – that is the goal of true education.'

– Martin Luther King Jr.

To answer this question we have to briefly return to January 1993, when Neil was appointed as Headteacher of West Kidlington School near Oxford. He has always enjoyed being a people watcher and was increasingly noticing that some pupils lacked any meaningful understanding about words such as respect, trust, honesty and humility – positive human values. Their behaviour witnessed this in their fractured relationships with their families and friends. Although they were great pupils in so many ways, he thought that if they were given access to the meaning of such words, and opportunities to think and practice living them, then there would be remarkable benefits for the pupils their families and the community. For instance, they would be more able to create a meaning and purpose for themselves, which would harness their creative energies, be more considerate and caring towards others and gain more from their school experience.

Neil shared this thinking and developed it with his colleagues and governors at the school, who gave him their full confidence and unconditional support to implement a form of values education and assess its success in a doctoral research study at Oxford University. Over seven years this values program was developed, refined and evaluated. The research evidence showed that the quality of education at the school improved. Ofsted confirmed this in their inspection report of the school in June 1997, which stated that the focus on values, which underpins all the work of the school, contributes directly to above average attainment, good progress, high standards of behaviour and excellent relationships. What had been achieved was an emotionally literate school. The values words also had a profound impact on staff both personally and professionally. The positive outcomes were there for all to see. Adults in the school became very aware that they had to model the values authentically, not always an easy option, so that pupils could see that what they said was also what they did as people – a key requirement of VbE. Linda Heppenstall, one of the teachers, said that she taught values through who she is – her attitude and behaviour. Linda understood that pupils absorb values in subtle ways not just through lessons. She made this point by saying:

'You do not actually have to teach a values lesson to impart values. You may not think you are teaching values but you are because that is who you are. Pupils take in what you want, what you stand for and the way you are with them.'

The research evidence showed that values education cannot be taught in isolation from the teacher's own thoughts, feelings and behaviour – their internal world.

As the values education program progressed it became apparent that the school was transforming the whole of its practice, developing a new educational philosophy and ways of working. Everything the school did through its curriculum, routines and culture was cross-referenced with the school's 22 community inspired values to ensure consistency. Consequently, what we describe as Values-based Education was born.

Today we use the following description to help people understand what Values-based Education is all about:

'VbE underpins the life and work of school communities, colleges, and other settings, including the home so that they are values-based. The term values-based implies that every aspect of life, both personal and professional is based on the way that values are lived. It is transformational, in that it invites cultural change that is based on equity and respect for all. It is challenging, as it calls us to ask what we can give to life, as opposed to what can we get from life?

'VbE promotes a way of being that values the self, others and the environment. It is simple: yet profound in its effects, it creates a calm and purposeful climate for learning. It is a developmental process that connects with the intrinsic qualities of human beings and actively nurtures them.'

Jane's background as a psychotherapist led her to be curious about what she observed in schools that had introduced VbE. She noticed that VbE created safe spaces, and in schools where all aspects of VbE – such as reflection – were being embraced, the adults and pupils had a heightened awareness of their inner world of thoughts and feelings. She was fascinated that VbE, without realising it, created a therapeutic healing environment in schools. Jane was excited to see that the positive energy, which is called self-energy, has a profound impact on wellbeing and resilience. Hence why we have spent the last few years forming what we now call the Inner Curriculum.

VbE views the purpose of education as the flourishing of humanity through Values-based Living. It is soundly based on research, which shows the positive effects on pupils, both socially and academically, when educators model and teach about universal, positive human values. The purpose of adopting VbE is to inspire young people to adopt positive values in their lives, to make them their virtues, so that they can be lifelong learners, developing wisdom, compassion, wellbeing and resilience, actively living the positive human values in their daily lives.

We think the following information about VbE may be helpful for you to use:

'Values-based Education happens when universal, positive human values explicitly underpin everything a school or any other organisation does.

'Values Education is any activity, which promotes the understanding of positive values, developing the habits, skills and dispositions of adults and pupils so they can live their values as active members of the community.

'Values are the key principles, which act as the general guides to our thinking and behaviour. They include: Peace, Justice, Respect, Love, Patience, Happiness, Caring, Trust, Honesty, Humility, Courage, Compassion, Tolerance and Hope. To a great extent our identity as people is determined by our values. If we radically change our values we can become 'different people'. To discover that someone's values are not as we thought they were is to discover that they are not the person we thought they were.

'The outcomes of VbE include pupils being more likely to develop positive character traits as they grow in values awareness. They become more emotionally literate and ethically intelligent – developing a strong moral compass. We observe that pupils are encouraged to develop a much-needed aptitude, which we have named as enhanced personal competence (EPC). EPC is the ability to be self-aware, working with complexity using a stable, positive and altruistic mindset. If you are in a VbE school or other setting you will see this aptitude being formed in your own pupils. We are sure you will be able to name many more positive outcomes, including VbE making the teaching and learning process more enjoyable for everyone; leading to Values-based Living.'

These points may be summed up in the words of Simon Cowley, the Director of a large Multi-Academy Trust, The White Horse Federation of Schools, who told us:

'Schools that successfully implement Values-based Education into the fabric of school life will reap the reward of providing students with a consistent approach to develop their social skills, this in turn benefitting their emotional wellbeing. One pupil's recent comment about the benefit of VbE resonates with me and justifies why the importance of reflective practices help our future generation develop in this ever changing world. The pupil told me: 'My values help me feel safe, when I am nervous or when I am not quite sure what to do next, I am able to apply my skills to reflect on reasons why. This helps me to pause, take my time and rationalise why I feel like this. This makes me feel more responsible for the decisions I am about to make and aware how it might also affect others. I often tell my mum about how the school values help me in life and we talk a lot about how this approach could help everyone else. I am going to take my values with me when I grow up to help others.

'The importance of Values-based Education is not just pupil centred but is for the school community as a whole. The structure of VbE in schools in our Trust has led to a more coordinated approach to the development of pupil's social and emotional wellbeing as well as teacher morale. A teacher recently commented about their first year experience of working in a VbE school: 'Happy teacher = happy children = a happy school. After working in my VbE school for just over a year now I can conclude that our 'values-based' approach is the glue of school life. It provides the structure to ensure pupils are fully aware of the connection and importance between academic and social and emotional learning in achieving their goals.'

The enthusiasm from Simon for VbE introduces us to our next chapter, which asks why should you be interested in VbE?

Chapter 2:
Why should you be interested in Values-based Education?

'When you teach your son, you teach your son's son.'

– Talmud rabbinical writings

This chapter explores the question, why you should be interested in VbE? Are values really that important? Shouldn't we all get on with aspects of the curriculum that are more beneficial to pupils i.e. the subjects in the curriculum?

Research evidence from teachers working in values-based schools indicates that although the formal curriculum is important, an emphasis on values is more important first. This is because a values-based classroom creates a unique climate for learning, one that is calm and purposeful, where good relationships based on mutual respect is the norm. It is where time and space is created for the person of the learner to feel safe and welcomed – an environment without fear or shame. Values create the opportunity for all to be self-analytical, rather than self-critical, curiosity being the driving force in the learning process.

The challenge for the adults in the school is to be seen by pupils as role models for the values. Research indicates that authentic modelling of positive values by staff has an encouraging and supportive influence on pupil behaviour, because pupils model their own behaviour on that of their teachers. Teachers who have enthusiastic positive attitudes, based on their values, give affirmation and positive reinforcement to the pupils.

Positive teacher behaviour is one of the most significant factors in affecting the climate for effective learning in the classroom. Teaching is more successful across the subjects of the curriculum when all teachers have a values focus for their lessons, being explicit about values no matter what lesson or area of study they are teaching. Teachers say that a class that has a values base to its discipline becomes easier to differentiate, so that pupils are more likely to get the most from the curriculum.

Marilyn Trigg, a teacher, gave us an example about the positive effect that values had in her class:

'It [values] has enabled my teaching to be more effective because the children concentrate more and they are more self-disciplined, so therefore I can actually differentiate much better. I can put them into groups and differentiate within the class much easier because the rest of the class are living our school values and are actually getting on and achieving, while I am teaching a small group of children.'

What other reasons may convince you to be fully engaged with VbE?

We are very concerned, as we are sure you must be, at the rise of mental health issues in schools and in society generally. This worrying point is made time and time again to us at teacher and headteacher conferences. Headteacher Jeff Conquest told us that in his Middle School (9-13) the effect of such things as cyber-bullying among pupils and parents spending less time with their children because of the demands of social media were having a negative impact on the wellbeing of his pupils.

Not only pupils feel increasingly stressed. We were asked to address a headteacher conference in the UK, to cheer up 50 headteachers who felt embattled with Ofsted feeling that they were being unfairly targeted. We listened for two hours as some of these heads displayed extreme anxiety

– one breaking down in tears. We did our best to raise morale but we came away believing that the inspection system had become counter-productive and that the school system could be more appropriately supported – as we had recently seen on a professional visit to Estonia – if there were a general focus on positive professional development. VbE focuses on the positive aspects of people and nurtures their development. This does not imply that it accepts mediocrity, on the contrary it sets high personal and systemic standards but in a way that nourishes rather than diminishes the human spirit.

Julie Rees, Headteacher of Ledbury Primary School in Herefordshire, is passionate about the positive effects of VbE on the wider school community. She told us:

'Values-based Education when it is truly embedded in a school community has a far-reaching impact on the wider community.

'At our school we have developed good relationships with parents in our community based on trust and honesty. We know that some of our parents are uneasy about coming into school because they may not have had good experiences with school when they were young, or they are nervous of the 'perceived' authority of teachers. Some parents come in for support (and a regular cup of tea) from our Wellbeing Coordinator, Carol. The impact of these meetings is positive for parents as they are valued and listened to, whilst their children benefit from the messages the parents receive.

'One of our parents, T, has had a tumultuous relationship with schools over the years, as a student herself and now, as a parent. T has experienced on-going mental health challenges, a series of difficult relationships and has experienced the sadness of losing a child. T's daughter, L, has been a motivated pupil at our school and has made excellent progress. She is a pupil who has fully embraced our motto, 'Determined to Succeed'.

'Last year T came to tell me that she was very excited because she had applied for her first job in a long time and she, like her daughter, was determined to succeed. Sure enough, after her interview T was offered the job and came to talk to me. She explained that the school had promoted a values-based ethos and she had learnt that valuing herself first was part of the role modelling she should show her daughter. T has two boys and two girls, their ages are between 4 and 13. T explained that she didn't want her 11-year-old daughter growing up and thinking that she had to follow in her mum's footsteps by having children from a young age. T recognised that L enjoyed her education and had many strengths across all subject areas, especially in maths and art. T explained that if she had a job, this was good modelling for her own children, especially her daughters; that having aspirations and the desire to work was positive. She thanked me for providing a values-based ethos that promoted valuing self. It gave her confidence to make positive changes.'

Julie's account gives an insight into why VbE is so successful, which is the focus of the next chapter.

Chapter 3:
What is the secret of Values-based Education's success?

'In a gentle way, you can shake the world.'

– Mahatma Gandhi

The secret of VbE's success is contained in its seven areas of transformational practice. They are not independent of each other as their unique blend creates the empowering process that schools find so successful. They are therefore introduced and developed simultaneously.

These seven aspects of VbE can be remembered by using the simple acronym MIRACLE. Initially we wondered if by using this word we would be in danger of causing offence by using a term that is usually associated with religion. However, after careful consideration and research we decided to use it, as a meaning of the word is marvelous example, which brilliantly describes the impact that the seven elements have on transforming school culture. Also, there is something about the nature of the word that makes it memorable and, therefore, fit-for-purpose.

Space in this section does not allow a full description and discussion of the seven aspects of VbE, but we hope the following brief descriptions will suffice in allowing you to sense their importance as transformational characteristics. Please remember that the elements are introduced simultaneously as they are inextricably intertwined and connected.

They are:

Modelling

Inner Curriculum

Reflection

Atmosphere

Curriculum

Leadership

Ethical Vocabulary

Let's consider briefly each of these elements:

Modelling: It is crucial that once a school has chosen its values then there is a searching discussion about how adults will authentically model them. Being a role model, is being a person looked on by others as an example to be imitated, implying being the sort of person you hope children will want to become. Carl Jung said: 'Children are educated by what the grown-up is and not by his talk.'

Being a role model is by no means a simple or easy task because, as the quote above suggests, it is demanding of our own energy. Also it is difficult because most of us have developed attitudes and ways of responding to others that are often outside of our conscious awareness. The way we develop over time is the product of so many factors, such as the way we were parented, the cultural and social groups to which we belong and the form of education that we have received. Being a values educator is not an easy option, requiring an openhearted curiosity and compassion about our own thinking and behaviour. Our aim is to be more self aware and conscious of the impact we have on others.

Effective modelling is dependant on good relationships, which are the bedrock of VbE, creating the energy that sustains positive values. Good relationship can be seen when adults are genuine; give unconditional positive regard and empathy to all pupils and each other. Adults who are able to connect to pupils, by attuning to the essence of who they are (not surface behaviours), have the most positive affect on student progress, achievement and social development. The outcome is secure adult-pupil attachment, which is similar to that of good parent-child attachment.

Such positive role modelling creates the energy for the establishment of attachment-based classrooms, where there is an emphasis on key conditions that are vital for learning. These being: ensuring teachers, like good parents, create positive attachment with their pupils; enable pupils to learn how to self-regulate their emotions and build self-esteem. Research, by Cozolino and others, explains how if these conditions are met then pupils develop secure attachment (comfortable in their own skins) with themselves and are able to be effective learners.

As adults work on modelling the values, we show children the adults that the world needs them to be. In turn, the children become role models too. At the Meads Primary School, Luton, UK, an eight-year-old girl proudly approached Neil holding a silver cup in her hands. Beaming with pride, she said, 'I've been given this cup, because I'm the class role model of the week.' Being a role model requires authentic self-awareness developed through reflective practice and an understanding of what we term the Inner Curriculum.

In our experience people who are good values role models have some, or occasionally all, of the following characteristics. We invite you to consider them in relation to yourself – some of the terms may be unfamiliar but will be explained later:

- Are values-aware and talk about them.
- Create attachment-based classrooms.
- Use a values vocabulary in daily life saying remarks such as, 'you showed respect.'
- Model values authentically – walk the talk. There is congruence between what is said and done.
- Display ethical intelligence when faced with dilemmas.
- Are self-aware.

- Make easy connections with pupils – great listeners, interested in the pupils as people, greet pupils to their class by shaking hands.
- Set clear and consistent boundaries for behaviour.
- Have smiling eyes, which indicate positive attitude, care and interest in others.
- Are emotionally intelligent.
- Have the ability to self-regulate emotions and feelings – mental integration.

How can we all develop the above so that we can consciously model positive values?

1. Remember that none of us are perfect – allow yourself to make mistakes – say sorry when you do.
2. Practice – have a value that you are thinking about and review your progress at the end of the day. Consider what impact it is having.
3. Ask colleagues and pupils for feedback.
4. As a family or staff work on the values, deepening understanding.
5. Praise modelling of values by your children/pupils.
6. Highlight good role models in sport, the arts and media.
7. Look for local examples of people who are good role models – invite them to share their experiences.
8. Consider allocating mentors to children who are good role models.
9. Catch children doing the right thing.
10. Be curious about challenging behaviours rather than critical.
11. Use expressions like, a part of you feels or behaves in that way, so that you avoid labelling the whole of a child.
12. Hold regular celebrations.
13. Express gratitude to your pupils. 'Thank you for the positive energy you put into our lesson.' If you model it they will then practice it too.
14. Look to hold regular real meetings with children so they feel that they are recognised, listened to and valued as people. In secondary schools, consider having three-party mentoring sessions

with students, one adult is the supervisor/manager; the other is the observer, support to the student. Student presents to the two adults about their progress and any issues that are inhibiting development.

15. Have class and/or school mantras that inspire children to do and be their best.

Next element of VbE for us to consider is the **Inner Curriculum**, which teaches us how to be aware and in control of our internal world of thoughts, feelings and emotions, enabling us to respond appropriately to others without hurting them or damaging our own sense of self. It enables pupils to be aware of any psychological blockages that may inhibit their relationships with others and their capacity to learn. A more comprehensive description will follow later. However, to get an overview you may like to watch and listen as Jane gives an introduction to the Inner Curriculum at a conference in Enfield. You can access the video on the VbE website at: www.valuesbasededucation.com

Now, **reflection**, which is a key component of the Inner Curriculum, is the means through which we access our internal world of thoughts, emotions, sensations and feelings, and regulate them, which helps us sustain mental health and increases the capacity for self-determination. We argue that this is a key skill for children to learn – the fourth 'R' of education. Reflective practices encompass a spectrum of activities including: thinking about your work; reflecting on our behaviour and the impact it has on other people; reflecting on a story and then maybe having an opportunity to discuss your thoughts with others and hear differing perspectives; mindfulness, silent sitting, visualisation and meditative practices. We will give you examples of practical exercises to help you develop inner stability through reflective practice later in this guide.

The term **atmosphere** encapsulates other descriptors, such as ethos and environment. It refers to the palpable ambience that characterises a VbE school, which Neil described in his book, *From My Heart: Transforming Lives Through Values* (Hawkes, 2013).

Atmosphere is deliberately created by a number of characteristics, which include:

- The quality of school displays; human-centric signage.
- Cleanliness.
- The quality, organisation and management of resources.
- The quality of the external environment – space for exercise and recreation.
- The calm working atmosphere, break time and quality of catering arrangements.
- How staff are valued and supported as people.
- Friendly and courteous behaviour of adults and children.

The atmosphere reflects the school's established culture and fully supports its curriculum.

Here are some examples, by no means an exhaustive list, which illustrate what a values-based atmosphere looks and feels like:

- It is calm and purposeful – tension-free.
- There is a natural emphasis on nurturing a healthy body, mind and spirit.
- By modelling the school's values a positive atmosphere is created.
- Everyone speaks respectfully to and about each other, all showing good manners.
- There is a focus on wellbeing and resilience.
- Signage is positive.
- The external environment is cared for and provides opportunities for exercise, recreation and love of nature.
- Photos of staff are not arranged in any hierarchical order but roles are clearly labelled. This shows that there is not a hierarchy of relationships, only a hierarchy of roles.
- Status is not rewarded by a bigger desk or easier car parking space.
- Answer phones have messages reflecting the values of the school.
- Reception and the school office are welcoming to everyone.
- There is an emphasis on maintaining physical health through healthy eating, drinking water and taking regular exercise.

- School meal times promote healthy eating and a pleasant social atmosphere.

- Values displays, external and internal, are creative and inspiring and contribute to the school's atmosphere.

- Members of staff create school routines, such as the movement of pupils around the school, in values awareness.

- Meaningful rituals are created that give a sense of pride in belonging to the school.

What can you do to review your own school's atmosphere?

We would suggest that you go through the aforementioned list at a staff meeting, incorporating a school walk where you bring the atmosphere of your school into sharp focus. Remember to be curious about your school rather than critical. This helps all to avoid retreating into defensiveness with remarks from colleagues such as: 'it's always been that way and it has worked!' Culture is deeply ingrained in a school so tread curiously, carefully and respectfully as you question the educational reason for an established routine.

Our next VbE element is **curriculum,** which refers to everything the school does to support VbE both implicitly, as described above in the description of atmosphere, and explicitly in ensuring that every aspect of the school's life and work reflects and is underpinned by the school's chosen values and the way that they are lived by the school community.

The school is clear about its meaning and purpose. It has a focus on wellbeing and building appropriate resilience in pupils. It enables pupils to be active agents, leaders of their learning. It sees the possibilities for growth in pupils rather than their limitations. All school policies are reviewed to ensure internal consistency with the school's values.

The curriculum encompasses the formal, informal and hidden curriculum. The formal curriculum, ensuring that values are explicitly and experientially taught about in lessons, not only discretely in values lessons but as an element in all aspects of the curriculum. The informal curriculum includes how break times are managed and resourced. The hidden curriculum reflects the school's culture and can be seen in the expectations (school uniform), routines (movement around the school) and practices (sports days, parent/staff meetings) of the school. All these aspects are considered to be the responsibility of the school's leadership.

The next part of MIRACLE is **leadership**. The leadership, in the person of the headteacher/principal, needs to feel convinced that VbE is relevant to achieving excellence and not merely a worthy extra, which diverts attention away from what is perceived to be the school's core purpose. The headteacher/principal is key, because he/she is the principle architect of the school's vision. We observe that having the capacity to dream big (using creative imagination) brings transformational positive energy (inspiration) into the formation of a VbE school – a prime characteristic of an altruistic leader. This, coupled with the seemingly endless capacity to access their own reservoir of uncontaminated self-energy, enables the leader(s) to remain stable and focused in an educational context of incomparable complexity and challenge. We have observed that the most effective schools enjoy distributed leadership where other staff share the leadership of the school; all staff being actively involved in creating the school's vision and development plans. In secondary education we have seen some outstanding examples of pupils taking active leadership roles in their schools.

During our VbE talks we always emphasise that the key capacity of the VbE leader(s) is to enable the release of the creative dynamic of everyone – quite a task! It is through their commitment, drive, care and their ability to inspire others that the leader(s) creates a sustainable school culture based on VbE, which has the active support of all members of staff. This ensures consistency of practice across all aspects of school life. Others will play a major part in the leadership of the school. However, we would argue that a VbE school encourages all members of the school, both adult and children, to be seen as leaders, taking personal responsibility for their thoughts and behaviour and sustaining an ethical vocabulary.

We invite you to consider the following information about what constitutes Values-based Leadership. We hope that it will give you a useful checklist against which you may consider the nature of leadership.

School leaders:

1. Take responsibility for developing, enabling and embedding a values framework that promotes wellbeing.
2. Cultivate the values and beliefs that create their own identity as leaders and drive their moral and professional purpose.
3. Inspire staff, pupils and parents to understand how values and their worldviews influence their relationships, thoughts, planning and ultimately their actions.
4. Gain commitment from all in the school's community by engaging them in a values framework that underpins the agenda for whole school growth and development.
5. Use inclusive processes to explore possibilities, dilemmas and challenges in achieving congruence between espoused values and actions, especially when faced with conflicting values and worldviews.
6. Work with staff to embed agreed values in what they do and how they do it to ensure that school culture has coherence; that pupils understand how critical values are to their present and future lives.
7. Establish, monitor, evaluate and refresh systems and processes to ensure that the school's values and beliefs are foundational to all aspects of teaching and learning, community development, strategic planning and organisational management.

Much has been written on leadership, but none better in our view than in the inspirational work of Floyd Woodrow who is an acknowledged outstanding leader. Floyd's work emphasises the importance of VbE as a critical aspect of leadership. Floyd has shown that a good leader is in possession of a compass for life. The compass may be briefly explained, with our interpretation, as follows but a full account can be found at www.compassforlife.co.uk.

A compass for life

As a leader (we are all leaders both children and adults), Floyd maintains that we need to be in possession of a compass for life. The north point of our compass represents our North Star, representing our mission, our meaning and purpose in life, our big ideas that we want to achieve on life's journey. Having clarity of purpose is vital for us all.

Next we look east to our ethos, our potential ethical intelligence, which comprises the values that we use in our life, which become our virtues. This is the moral side of our compass, which we believe embraces all that we promote in Values-based Education.

Opposite east is west, the good warrior, full of wisdom who has developed character traits based on the values of the east point of the compass. We think that these dispositions, virtues, allow us to achieve our purpose in life, ensuring that we don't suffer from having an existential vacuum – a life without meaning. We think that this is where self-energy, the life force, the innate energy and the essence of humanity that fosters health and healing, resides.

Lastly, we look south to the point of strategy. We may have a wonderful vision but unless we think how to achieve our vision and have appropriate strategies and action then little will be accomplished.

We do commend this compass for life model, which we believe is at one level so easy to remember but so profound in its application. Children of all ages will love it too.

The final letter of MIRACLE represents the **ethical vocabulary** that the school makes explicit in its life and work. Although last in the MIRACLE list, it is of prime importance as the foundation of VbE was built on it. When setting out on the VbE journey the initial focus of VbE is on the selection, practice and living of an ethical vocabulary.

The ethical vocabulary comprises a community chosen set of universal, positive human values such as respect, tolerance, resilience, determination, courage, integrity and compassion. A distinction is clearly made between these positive human values and those that limit our potential such as greed, envy, intolerance and indoctrination.

We always emphasise that it is important to select a wide range of positive values (principles that guide our thinking and behaviour): primary schools often choose to have 22, which they explicitly focus on, one a month, over a two-year cycle in assemblies and experiential lessons. Each time a value is encountered it is considered at greater depth. All the values are used implicitly at every opportunity, reinforcing values-based behaviour. For example, a teacher may remark to a group, 'well done for cooperating and showing respect for one another'.

Secondary schools build on this foundation, extending the pupils understanding of values by considering ethical dilemmas and putting the values into action through community service projects. Values may be known by other terms such as heart strengths, virtues or character traits. Each subject area ensures that values are highlighted in lesson planning. We have seen excellent examples during lessons in physical education, mathematics, science, English, art and the humanities. Student voice is also an active way of engaging young people in a values dynamic. We have watched outstanding presentations by students who are using their voice to draw attention to unethical aspects of life. A group of students touched our hearts when they gave a presentation on human rights in El Salvador. Another example was at Levenshulme High School in Manchester where the students were actively working with the staff to create a school of excellence.

The selection of positive values words finds universal support from all the major world religions and non-religious groups. These values, when actively lived by people, become their character traits or virtues (values in action). We believe that they help children to develop what we have termed ethical intelligence (EI), which we argue is the most important of all the intelligences to nurture, as it is through EI that human beings can come together to solve world problems. This, we reason, is because the development of an ethical vocabulary enhances and enriches communicative competence, which we maintain could lead to a new universal narrative, problem solving language, based on common values.

These principles and practices of VbE have touched the imagination of a range of schools throughout the world and consultants are working to help school leaders embed VbE in the context of their own schools and countries. For instance, VbE Consultant Pat Beechey, has recently worked in Nigeria, introducing Values-based Education. VbE was approached with a request to provide support to the Foundation for Values Transformation (FVT), to introduce and establish Values-based Education into the state education system in Lagos, Nigeria.

FVT is a charity based in Lagos that has striven to obtain funding in order to work with schools in establishing a values ethos in their staff and pupils. FVT believe that if pupils are introduced to values and receive an education that both promotes and establishes ethical behaviour, these attitudes will stay with students and filter into the work place at all levels. Given the political and social climate in Nigeria, this is an aim of gargantuan proportions. However, they believe that despite the enormity of the task – e.g. a population of 188 million with a growth rate of 2.56% – it is set to overtake USA in mid-2020s, that with determination it can succeed.

The delegates gave Pat an outstanding evaluation on the effectiveness of her VbE training. Olawega, one of the delegates summed up the training, 'Yes we can and yes we will!'.

Pat's work is based on a values blueprint, which you will find at www. valuesbasededucation.com. Also, we think it is worth emphasising again that the elements of MIRACLE are introduced seamlessly, building on each other and creating a place for people, both young and old, to flourish.

We hope that in the above paragraphs we have given you enough information and examples so that you can see why VbE is so transformational. It is an educational paradigm that challenges the traditional cultural norm of schooling, aiming to empower young people to nurture their inner innate qualities – values making them their virtues. You can find lots of help and support by visiting www. valuesbasededucation.com.

As you can sense, VbE invites us to consider our relationships with others and uniquely with ourselves. This is why an outcome, as well as a transformational ingredient, of VbE is the Inner Curriculum.

Chapter 4:
What is the Inner Curriculum?

'Man cannot be free unless he is master of himself.'

– Epictetus, Greece AD55-35

In the previous chapter, we explained that the Inner Curriculum is a part of the seven elements of VbE (MIRACLE). The Inner Curriculum is being recognised as one of the powerful transformational aspects of VbE, which we now understand to be both a natural outcome when schools develop VbE, and of profound importance in its own right. Earlier we stated that the Inner Curriculum teaches us how to be aware and in control of our internal world of thoughts, feelings, sensations and emotions, enabling us to respond appropriately to others without hurting them or damaging our own sense of self.

What we have observed and learned in our work with values-based schools is that the Inner Curriculum nurtures a secure sense of our authentic self, the spiritual essence of who we are, profoundly enhancing our feeling of wellbeing and our ability to be resilient. The transformational properties of the Inner Curriculum may also be likened to and found in a number of therapeutic theories and related practices such as: Interpersonal Neurobiology, Transactional Analysis (TA), the Internal Family System (IFS), Mindfulness, Myers-Briggs Personality

Types, Carl Roger's Person Centred Psychotherapy, the works of Carl Jung and Emotion Coaching – to name just a few. We believe that an insight into these theories enhances the positive outcomes of the Inner Curriculum, enabling the advancement of a new understanding of pro-social human consciousness, which promotes personal and social health. The Inner Curriculum brings together Education, Interpersonal Neurobiology, Psychotherapy and the wisdom of humanity in a new dynamic relationship that enhances both learning and wellbeing. We want to share with you some of our ideas and thinking that we are developing alongside colleagues who are experts in these fields.

To explain: if the principles and practices of VbE are naturally, without coercion, embedded in a culture, whether in a home, school or other system then the conditions are naturally created, which nurture and support the quality of our internal worlds. This process gives us greater self-awareness, emotional literacy and ethical intelligence. For instance, if children have the opportunity to think about the value of respect, by practicing showing respect in real situations in their lives, then gradually this concept of respect is embedded in their brains and emerges as one of their character traits, habits, which we can also describe as one of their virtues.

An aim of VbE is therefore to promote a school and home ethos that nourishes children's innate positive qualities from an early age. VbE nurtures the development of a child's pro-social behaviour, creating a mindset that is more likely to be prone to compassion and altruism.

The education system has always had an external curriculum of subjects, themes and dimensions but it has rarely foreground the internal world of the student as an equal partner in the educative process. Hence why we maintain that there is an urgent need for an inner curriculum that takes account of a person's inner world, which can promote or inhibit an individual's capacity to learn and form relationship with themselves and others.

Until comparatively recently, it was assumed that children were like empty bottles that needed to be filled with facts and information. It was also presumed that all children, unless they were children with special needs, if given the right teaching could achieve similar standards and outcomes (aspects of this thinking survive today). Scant, if any, regard was given to what children bring to school in terms of their thinking, feelings, emotions, sensations and fantasies and how these impact on their ability to be both successful learners and have what we call a secure sense of self. They are able to express one of the fundamental beliefs of Transactional Analysis (TA), which is expressed as, 'I'm OK and you are OK'.

We are convinced, from the evidence we have from VbE schools, that thinking about values becomes a creative, driving energy that informs and strengthens our wellbeing, as it helps us to understand ourselves – a unique outcome.

How? The answer lies in the understanding that VbE does not pathologise – looking for what's wrong with a person but instead concentrates on what it means to be human. About the same time as Neil and his colleagues were developing VbE at West Kidlington School, neuroscientists were gaining new insights into the working of the human brain. At the time, they were not aware of these neurological advances and that VbE was suggesting ways of being and learning that supported these new scientific findings.

VbE uses the healing energy of positive values and relationships to inform the way we think and behave, which supports what we see as our innate capacities. For instance, neurobiology teaches us that the human being is hard wired to be cooperative and trusting. This is a biological imperative from our ancestral past when survival depended on members of a tribe being able to cooperate, which can still be observed in babies and young children. VbE supports these innate capacities, helping us not to action thoughts that may be harmful to us. Our ancestors needed these responses in order to survive but in the 21st century they often harm us. For instance, if someone upsets us to the point of feeling overwhelmed by fear, anger or any emotion, the body responds by producing chemical responses in the form of adrenalin or the harmful increase of cortisol. The results affect our immune system and our thinking processes are impaired. In these circumstances our ancestors would have gone into flight, fight or freeze/flop mode, but in the office environment, school or home we have to sit and literally stew in our own emotions.

For children who live in homes that are stressful, when they come into school small things can overwhelm them because they are on high alert. In a VbE school that is calm and purposeful, consistent, trusting and relational, their system can relax and they can then begin to experience themselves in a self-enhancing way. This process takes time to internalize and, in extreme cases, the children need the support of a small nurture group with adults who are loving, non-judgemental and set consistent boundaries.

We all need to learn how to keep our internal world healthy, despite what is happening around us. We learn through the Inner Curriculum that we can be an objective observer of the drama of life, which we see and are involved in. Helping children to understand that they have a choice in their responses is key to them understanding how to self-regulate their reactions to thoughts and attendant emotions in order to stay mentally calm and healthy.

A simple practical technique is to teach children the wisdom cycle. In the wisdom cycle we create a mental pause between an external stimulus, such as someone asking us a question or our need to respond to a situation. This pause allows us to consider all factors and sense our priorities for an accurate response. Neil once asked Emily, a young seven year old who was showing him around a school, how she calmed herself down. She naturally went into the wisdom cycle: she placed her finger on her lips, averted her gaze, went internal for a couple of seconds and then, looking up, replied: 'I think of peace.'

VbE supports the healthy development of our mental capacities. Given the space, time and supportive relationships, we can guide ourselves to a more enhanced state of wellbeing, resilience and happiness. The reason for this is that we already have the natural capacity to nourish these qualities within us.

Happiness (a sense of flourishing) is not something that's out there in the world for us to find, like a birthday present; it is actually an innate aspect of humanity – we all have it. However, many of us don't know this because it isn't something that we are taught in the school curriculum or generally learn from our family or society. In fact we often learn the opposite in myths such as work hard, achieve qualifications, get a great job, gain wealth and power and you will be happy. No one wants to be poor but there is a balance that we must achieve if our specie is to survive.

There is a wonderful ancient story, called The Secret, which helps to illustrate the point we are making.

'Once upon a time the gods were wondering where they could hide the secret of peace and joy. They didn't want humans to find the secret until they had matured enough to appreciate it. It was suggested by one god that it should be hidden in the highest mountain. This idea was rejected as too easy a place to search, as was the dense forest. The wisest god who had been in deep thought suggested to his fellow gods that they hide the secret in the human heart, which he said was the last place that they would look! They all agreed and there the secret has remained because we never think to search for peace and joy in our hearts. We look everywhere else, in relationships, careers, travel, self-help groups and gurus.'

The story illustrates that we human beings habitually look for the sources of happiness in the external world rather than realising that they are within us. The Greeks coined the word *eudemonia*, which means *human flourishing*, which we think extends the concept of happiness to one that is more encompassing of our global community.

The Inner Curriculum contains the processes for helping us to appreciate our innate spiritual qualities and to manifest them in our lives, thereby experiencing wellbeing. In doing so, we release our core self that can remain stable during the ups and downs of daily living.

Let's now look further at our definition of the Inner Curriculum, which we hope will be useful to you in school or at home. Some of the language may, at first sight, appear unfamiliar:

'The Inner Curriculum teaches us how to be conscious about and in harmonious control of our internal spiritual world of thoughts, feelings and emotions, enabling us to respond appropriately and altruistically to others without hurting them or damaging our own sense of self. Indeed it supports the development of a strong and secure sense of self, which develops the disposition of self-leadership, which sustains wellbeing.

'We define self to be the innate essence of human consciousness, the 'you' who is observing, a healing energy that creates the space for the nurturing of wisdom. When we experience self-energy we are accessing our authentic nature.

'We argue passionately that a core objective of education should be to nurture self-energy, in the context of thinking about and applying human values such as empathy, courage, resilience, altruism, peace, generosity and justice. Such virtues are often evident when there is a natural disaster or major catastrophe, but sadly these are not universally seen during normal life. We think that VbE schools and others, which care deeply about the character development of people, bring such traits into consciousness.

'The Inner Curriculum evolves in a calm and purposeful environment, one that allows the authentic self to flourish. When our self-energy is leading our internal world then we, and others, have the potential to experience wellbeing and release our innate creativity and connectedness. Self-energy is contagious as it makes it safe for this quality to emerge in others. As humanity shares this simple yet profound wisdom, we hope that it will produce leaders with the new intelligence to solve the complex problems we face in our world.'

Concluding thoughts...

A knowledge and understanding of the elements of the Inner Curriculum enables each one of us to respond appropriately to others without hurting their feelings or making us feel unhappy by damaging our own sense of self. Indeed the Inner Curriculum supports the development of a strong and secure sense of self, which develops a disposition we have called self-leadership (agency), which sustains wellbeing. As we have more self-energy we naturally become less judgemental, are more compassionate and are able to feel a greater connection with others.

As you will probably be aware, unconscious processes govern most of our responses to life's events; we so often sail through the day on automatic pilot. How much of your day can you recall right now? Are there some aspects of today that you would have liked to respond to differently? How spontaneous or reflective have you been?

As we have stated, the outcome of the Inner Curriculum is wellbeing. This includes enabling pupils to be resilient and less susceptible to mental illness. It also ensures that they gain more from the curriculum, as they have greater personal control over their learning and behaviour.

We hope by this stage in this guide we have given you enough insight so that you can feel as excited about the potential of the Inner Curriculum as we are. We are sure you have many questions that we are always pleased to answer. However, we hope many of your queries will be answered in our next section, which is about how you support the development of the Inner Curriculum? What do you need to know? What strategies will help you design the Inner Curriculum in your school or home? Let's now consider the practicalities.

Part B:
How to Develop the
Inner Curriculum

Chapter 1:
Important introductory remarks

'Knowing yourself is the beginning of all wisdom.'

– Aristotle

As previously mentioned, the Inner Curriculum teaches us how to be aware and in control of our internal world of thoughts, feelings, sensations and emotions, enabling us to respond appropriately to others without hurting them or damaging our own sense of self. Jane was intrigued when she noticed that IC when spoken aloud becomes 'I see' or 'Eye See', which is what happens when we understand the insights that the Inner Curriculum gives us.

When we create the right values-based environment, it nourishes students' mental health, empowering their brains to remedy pathways that are holding them back. It equips staff with new tools, with new insights, into responding to challenging behaviour, even the most challenging behaviour, in ways that support students to be able to respond in more appropriate ways to stresses they are otherwise unable to cope with.

The principles behind the Inner Curriculum are drawn from a variety of sources taken from disciplines, such as Interpersonal Neurobiology; Transactional Analysis; the Internal Family System; Polyvagal theory;

play, drama and art therapies; Philosophy for Children (P4C) and aspects of the formal curriculum that covers pupils' spiritual, moral, social and cultural development (SMSC), personal, social and health education (PSHE), emotional literacy, values mentoring, emotion coaching, counselling and importantly silent sitting, reflection and mindfulness. If you want to extend and deepen your knowledge, the internet is filled with wonderful and relevant resources that you will find fascinating.

A health warning

Please be mindful that in entering into your own inner world and those of others, care should be taken only to use our suggestions as far as they are supportive and helpful. If you sense that you or another requires professional support from a doctor, qualified counsellor, mentor or psychotherapist then please seek help. We estimate that the Inner Curriculum's techniques and tools are safe and appropriate for the majority of people but there is a small percentage, which perhaps because of their challenging life history, behaviour or personality, should seek the support of qualified specialists. Please may we make it clear that our suggestions are to support classroom teachers and support staff to help pupils thrive: it is not intended to be a professional manual for mental health professionals working with children diagnosed with mental illness.

Please also consider your own range of interpersonal skills, being as honest as you can about your level of emotional literacy. This means that you will objectively assess your capacity and willingness to compassionately attune to the internal world of another. You may conclude that others are more suitable to undertake the Inner Curriculum. We state this not to discourage you, on the contrary, but we are aware that the Inner Curriculum is most effective when being implemented by someone who is self-aware, able to attune to others and curious about his or her own mental and emotional processes that make up the internal world. When working with others it is vital that a safe space is created for the work, which gives permission to the internal world to show itself authentically. The person conducting the Inner Curriculum activities should be seen as an integral part of this safe space. If you are unsure if this work is for you then we suggest that you talk to a person whom you trust and who will give you honest and constructive feedback.

By now you will have understood that the Inner Curriculum, at a general level, is an outcome of VbE, i.e. adults and young people become more self-aware of their thoughts and the values that drive their behaviour. However, to allow both our pupils and ourselves to understand our internal world (gaining an understanding and ability to be the leader of it) we draw on a variety of sources that will be acknowledged in the text and in the suggested reading. We would like to acknowledge our deep sense of gratitude to the range of scholars and practitioners who have made the formation of the Inner Curriculum possible. We believe that what you are reading represents work in progress and will be revised as we gain further insights and evidence from research.

We realise too that schools have not generally been given some basic tools to develop the Inner Curriculum so we hope that the following section will support you. We are aware that you may like to have training in these aspects so please contact us through the contact section of www. valuesbasededucation.com for further support. We are interested in your feedback, and we will value it too.

Chapter 2:
The starting point for the Inner Curriculum

'Who looks outside, dreams; who looks inside awakes.'

– Carl Jung

The starting point for the Inner Curriculum begins with you! Before you work with anyone else please spend time becoming familiar with, and using the tools yourself. It is helpful in the process of understanding the elements if you are able to share your experience of working with the Inner Curriculum with others. For instance, by forming a team to act as a supervision or peer group, in which you can share your experiences in a non-judgemental way and have others comment on them.

A primary school headteacher recently shared with us that her staff all enthusiastically supported VbE. However, a few of them found it difficult to manage children with Special Educational Needs (SEN), especially those with conditions such as autism and ADHD. She said that the teachers appeared to be afraid of the children. We suspect that this is not an isolated case and reveals one of our concerns, which is that some adults find it very difficult to form positive relationships with so called challenging children because, at a neurological level, their anxiety is transmitted to the children which makes them feel unsafe and anxious too.

It is not only when staff feel afraid, that the importance of relationships are overlooked. Sometimes the importance of what may appear as mundane routine activities is underestimated. At a staff training day in London, a headteacher of a special school asked Jane to remind staff to remember that whatever they were doing with one of the pupils was the most important activity at that moment. The headteacher had noticed that staff would often be hurried whilst attending to such natural activities as assisting a child who needed help with toileting. They had a mindset that there were more important things to do. She wanted them to understand that of prime importance was the connection and relationships they were developing in every aspect of the child's time at school.

An understanding of Dr. Stephen Porges' Polyvagal theory may be helpful if you recognise aspects of yourself in the previous paragraphs. The theory, widely applauded by neuroscientists and psychotherapists, describes the functions of the 10th cranial nerve, the vagus, which has two distinct branches, each developed at different periods of our evolution. The evolutionary newer mammalian branch helps in the establishment of caring relationships, but if we are stressed and worried then the older reptilian branch, which Dr. Porges likens to a turtle, becomes dominant and shuts down positive emotion.

In the classroom this may mean that we are unable to relate to a child who is stressed and unhappy because our responses communicate our own fear. This is despite trying to smile and remain calm; the key is always in our eyes. The newer branch of the vagus nerve connects with the upper face and if switched on through positive experience will communicate safety and trust to the pupil. That is why Neil has always emphasised the importance of having smiling eyes, which in the words of Carl Rogers – a highly respected psychotherapist – transmits unconditional positive regard, empathy and genuineness. Research is showing that people who practice mindfulness are more likely to be influenced by the newer branch of the vagus nerve. For children this knowledge helps their personal, social development. For adults it reinforces the importance of creating a nurturing environment that supports the establishment of good relationships, which are the key to learning.

Before reading further, may we invite you to pause and consider the quality of the relationships that you have with children?

Do you find it easy to connect with children? Do you sense that children warm to you? What is it about your personality that nurtures good relationships? Do the same children respond differently with others? Do you sometimes feel afraid that children will not do as you ask them? How do you feel when you sense you are having a positive relational experience?

We have watched countless teachers and support staff interacting with children and are continually fascinated to observe how some people seem to establish good relationships effortlessly whilst others find it difficult and, in rare cases, makes them unsuitable to work with children. Fear is one emotion that inhibits relationship building. The following two examples help to explain what we mean:

A headteacher of a large primary school, in a challenging urban social environment, shared with us a traumatic incident that had happened to one of her more disadvantaged pupils on a transition day to a secondary school. The boy, who we will call Dave, lived on a social housing estate with his grandparents. His mother was a drug dealer and his dad was in prison so the grandparents had taken the boy into their home. Dave had been placed in a nurture group and the school's staff had spared no effort to create a secure environment in which he could begin to trust adults. He had made good progress, although from time-to-time he 'lost it' with other children and adults. In the community he was an active part of a gang culture.

On arrival at the secondary school he had held his behaviour together until break time when he and a friend started play fighting. Dave accidently kicked his friend, who immediately screamed out in pain and then went to report the incident. A member of staff then shouted at Dave who immediately told the adult to f*** off. From then on the tension escalated as a senior leader in the school approached and, in exerting his authority, asked Dave whether he wanted to come to the school next term? 'I f****** well don't', came the angry response. Subsequently, Dave was told that he wouldn't last a day next term before he's excluded.

The primary school headteacher was summoned to take Dave back to the primary school, without completing his induction day. The headteacher said that the transition process for such children often dooms them to failure because the complexity of their needs is not understood and their behaviour induces fear and inappropriate adult responses. The headteacher further explained that Dave felt frightened, cornered, being in an unfamiliar setting, where the volume of all his defenses were turned up.

We are wondering what reactions you have had to this example?

May we invite you to pause and consider your thoughts about the two schools and Dave?

If you were a teacher what would you have done in similar circumstances if you were working in the primary or secondary school? Are transitions for such pupils bound to be traumatic experiences?

We guess that your thoughts will be based on your experience of, and attitudes to children who have challenging behaviours.

What we can assume from our basic knowledge of neuroscience is that Dave's brain's limbic system, a part of which is his amygdala (the fear centre), had been emotionally hijacked, creating an extreme emotional response – in other words, he lost his self-control. Members of staff probably felt their own fear too and then became angry, attempting to control Dave's behaviour by being authoritarian and confrontational.

This example demonstrates how we all need to be mindful when putting either others or ourselves into unfamiliar situations. We are sure that you can recall a time when you were placed in a new setting and felt distressed or uncertain. This happens because a younger less mature part of us may feel overwhelmed. In Dave's case the volume is turned up to such a degree that he didn't have enough self-energy to cope. We wonder if the primary school had adequately prepared Dave for the day? Had they unintentionally set him up to fail?

At his new school, having become very disturbed, Dave was not provided with an appropriate space and adequate time to calm down. No familiar, trusted adults were present to support him. If there had been, they could have used a calming technique, suggested by the renown American psychologist and neuroscientist, Louis Cozolino, who suggests we become, 'amygdala whisperers', using our warmth, empathic caring and positive regard to decrease the fear and distress that amygdala activation creates in pupils. Such calming behaviour, Cozolino suggests, creates in pupils a state of mind that increases neuroplasticity and learning.

Let us briefly consider what neuroplasticity is and its implications for education. The concept of stimulating neuroplasticity is very important in the brain conscious classroom. This is because such a classroom is aware of the brain's ability to reorganise itself by forming new neural connections throughout life. Neuroplasticity allows the neurons (nerve cells) in the brain to compensate for injury and disease. It is important, for those of us who teach or support learning, to know the importance of creating new learning opportunities that are high in challenge and low in stress, which will stimulate new neural growth. This means that the neurons in the brain are given opportunities to change both their structure and relationship to one another through new experiences. Thus the VbE classroom aims to create a learning environment that provides rich opportunities for greater neuroplasticity – a growth mindset.

Returning to our consideration of Dave: the primary school headteacher felt the system had let Dave down and that all the work of her staff was being undone. She predicted that Dave would be excluded on his first day at the secondary school and that he would follow the path of his father by ultimately being put in prison. She felt very sad for Dave.

The story may seem extreme and we are not recounting this story intending to be judgemental about either the primary or secondary school. What we hope the case study illustrates is that the induction process did not take account of children such as Dave, which led to a total breakdown in relationships. We are aware that such children struggle to conform to an established school culture, as they create challenges that, unless responded to appropriately, will end in school exclusion.

The second example, with a focus on relationships, is based on a recent experience Neil had when conducting an audit for the Enhanced Values Quality Mark at Wilds Lodge Therapeutic School in Rutland. This is a school that specialises in nurturing and teaching boys (aged 7-18) with autism, ADHD and other similar conditions that impact on behaviour.

The driving force of the school's pedagogy is good relationships. The staff team spare no amount of effort to gain the trust, respect and confidence of the pupils. Neil observed an outstanding Key Stage 2 nurture group session with Cherida Gibson who demonstrated how the six principles of nurture are being combined with a VbE approach to learning. The Nurture Group Network define the six principles of nurture as:

1.   Children's learning is understood developmentally.
2.   The classroom offers a safe base.
3.   The importance of nurture for the development of wellbeing.
4.   Language is a vital means of communication.
5.   All behaviour is communication.
6.   The importance of transition in children's lives.

Good manners was the current focus value and the group of Key Stage 2 pupils were invited to consider a range of behaviours and words, expressed through puppets, choosing which examples were good or bad manners.

Good manners are codified so that pupils know what is expected of them and were clearly evident throughout the day. An outstanding example is the way that meal times are conducted with pupils and staff sharing delicious home cooked food in a system of family service that develops responsibility, respect and courtesy. Members of staff act as great role models and give every opportunity for the pupils to develop conversational skills. The staff know the pupils really well and have built secure attachment, expressed in terms of meaningful relationships which engender trust and feelings of safety. Underpinning this is the way that members of staff deeply and attentively listen to both what pupils are saying, and what they are communicating through their body language. Such interpersonal competencies are well honed at Wilds Lodge School. Neil observed that staff were authentic and genuine people who share who they are and their interests with the pupils. This has a profound effect on building self-confidence and respectful relationships. If a pupil is in need of support because they feel emotionally overwhelmed, they are held in a safe and secure environment knowing that staff really do care and value them.

Pupils are constantly faced with dilemmas related to their own behaviour as well as in the formal curriculum. Pupils are invited to think about their behaviour in a non-judgemental way, which helps them to develop the skills associated with self-regulation and self-leadership.

May we invite you again to pause and consider this school's practice?

Is such practice only possible in a special school with specialist staff that is trained in the skills of forming relationships with children with challenging behaviour?

We know Wilds Lodge School well, having been regular visitors, and the school underpins all its work with VbE and uses aspects of the Inner Curriculum to enable students to self-regulate their behaviour. The school ensures that pupils have opportunities to consciously think and talk about painful experiences so that events can be placed in a coherent narrative. This process gives them the ability to heal trauma by naming the pain thereby decreasing it and promoting healing.

Watching the school's pupils on one of their public events, such as their annual music festival, when pupils from local schools are invited to take part, it would be very difficult to identify which children are deemed to have behaviour problems. Consistent relationships and safe boundaries enable the pupils' defense systems to settle and self-control to be established. This takes a lot of time and patience, within routines and structures that are designed to enable the pupil to connect with the adults.

We hope these two contrasting case studies will help you understand why we consider that the most important element in the Inner Curriculum is you; your natural ability to form appropriate relationships with young people, underpinned by a basic understanding of therapeutic processes.

In writing about these case studies we are concerned that we may give an unintended impression that the Inner Curriculum is only for reaching children who have more extreme behaviours. On the contrary, we think that all who work with and/or care for children will be able to enhance their relationships through the Inner Curriculum. Neil can recall on his own experience as a headteacher when he and his colleagues created a values-based school in Oxfordshire – the calm and purposeful atmosphere was palpable.

The local council wanted to place a boy, who had been excluded from other mainstream schools, in the school. The boy called Dirk and his parents came to see if our school would be appropriate for him. They explained that Dirk's experience of school had been traumatic but they wondered if he would settle and learn in ours?

Dirk presented himself as a sullen, willful boy who obviously didn't trust people in schools. The parents obviously loved him but seemed to have little control over his behaviour. They said that when Dirk was born he was ill and a lot of his early childhood experiences had been in having regular visits to the hospital. He was also born in the summer, which they felt had disadvantaged his early progress in school. They said that he quickly became angry and frustrated when not getting his own way and that a previous school had labeled him as having ADHD.

After consulting key teaching and support staff, Neil agreed that Dirk could come to the school, initially for a trial period of a month, to allow for a proper assessment. Also for both school and home to agree that the school was the most appropriate one for Dirk's needs. Neil said that we would form a partnership with the parents so that they could come to understand the methods that we would use and then use them at home too. He said that he would like them to spend time in the school, not observing Dirk, but seeing how we create a values-driven school culture.

When Dirk initially joined the school, his body language was of a person about to explode. Neil observed him in the playground, but the thing he noticed most was the behaviour of other pupils; they didn't respond to Dirk's challenges. Occasionally the adult assigned to form a positive attachment with Dirk had to draw his attention away from situations that would have led to him 'losing it'.

Dirk was placed in a nurture group where he could form relationships with a small group of people. At the end of the month we were pleased that all parties agreed that Dirk could stay. The parents fulfilled their side of the bargain, which included never criticising the school in front of Dirk, which Neil suspected had been happening when he attended previous schools.

Let us now fast-forward a year: Neil does not pretend that Dirk's journey was all positive, as days had their ups and downs. However, observing Dirk in the playground you would not have singled him out as different from the other children in terms of his behaviour. The other pupils and staff had acted as great role models and consequently Dirk let go of his fear and started to trust. We had shown that the strategies that are paramount in VbE could have a profound effect on most children, which is why we recommend the practices to all schools, colleges and other settings.

We have identified the value of trust as being a key ingredient in a school or other setting. When we visited Madley school in Herefordshire we were shown round the school by a boy who had only been in the school for a few months. He told us that in his previous school he was very badly behaved and would be sent to a room to sit by himself. He hated the school and his parents transferred him to Madley. He talked glowingly about the headteacher and how things were completely different here. He wasn't treated as a naughty boy and had been given responsibilities, which he loved. He said nobody wanted to listen to him at the other school but here both adults and pupils seemed to care for each other. There was no doubt that in this school developing good relationships was the bedrock on which the creative and experiential curriculum sat.

Having established the primacy of forming good relationships, we will now explain the key elements of the Inner Curriculum, which are:

- Getting to know your brain.

- Exploring reflective practices.

- The Internal Family System: a method that help us understand our internal world.

- More useful activities that will help you develop an Inner Curriculum.

In each of these three sections we will give a short introduction and then a number of tools/exercises for you to use.

Chapter 3:
Getting to know your brain

'Rabbit's clever,' said Pooh thoughtfully.
'Yes,' said Piglet, 'Rabbit's clever.'
'And he has Brain.'
'Yes,' said Piglet, 'Rabbit has Brain.'
There was a long silence.
'I suppose,' said Pooh, 'that that's why he never understands anything.'

– A. A. Milne, Winnie-the-Pooh

Over the last 20 years there has been tremendous growth in the understanding of the structure and workings of the human brain. We want to acknowledge that it is easy for us, who are not experts in the field, to over simplify and make assumptions that some scientists may rightly challenge. Therefore, we have been careful to give you as accurate an introduction as possible, but please be aware that new understandings are emerging about the science of the brain.

A number of years ago we were introduced to the outstanding work of Dr. Dan Siegel, who is one of the world's driving forces behind a science of the brain, known as Interpersonal Neurobiology. Dan researches the structure of the human brain and its relationship with the mind, which he describes as a relational process.

We passionately believe that all children should have an understanding, based on their age and stage, of the main parts of the human brain and how they influence their thinking and behaviour. Such an understanding strengthens the ability to work on that part of The Inner Curriculum, which is about recognising that we can take control of our thoughts and responses by growing new neurons (neurogenesis) that will positively affect our level of wellbeing.

One of the keys for enhancing learning at home or in the classroom is to be aware of a concept called neuroplasticity, which is the brain's ability to reorganise itself by forming new neural connections throughout life. Neuroplasticity allows the neurons (nerve cells) in the brain to compensate for injury and disease and also to adjust their activities in response to new situations or to changes in their environment. We now have an understanding about how neurons have the ability to change both their structure and relationship to one another through experience. This means that a good classroom gives pupils experiences that nurture greater neuroplasticity.

Laughter and appropriate humour is one aspect of VbE because it stimulates neuroplasticity. It improves memory recall, increases attention, reduces anxiety, improves self-esteem and activates brain growth hormones – to name but a few of the benefits. Therefore, we recommend that schools and homes becomes brain aware, by understanding the optimal conditions for learning that the brain requires.

We have been amazed how children as young as six can begin to have awareness that they have a brain that is comprised of various parts that have distinct functions. As children mature they can grasp the more technical aspects of the brain's structure and functioning. With this knowledge they will begin to appreciate the limitless potential of their brains.

Alongside knowing the brain's structure and its functions, we think it is important for children and parents to understand how to keep their brains healthy. There are four key ways of caring for the brain: right food, regular exercise, reflective practices and rest – the four R's. Research shows that when any or all of these four are lacking then the health and growth of the brain is impaired, as is the person's sense of wellbeing and their ability to be resilient. For instance, a healthy breakfast is important as it promotes learning. In his book Tricky Teens, Andrew Fuller, clinical child psychologist, recommends eggs for breakfast especially on exam days for teenagers. This is because the protein in eggs is quickly absorbed into the brain to aid thinking. Exercise increases the blood supply to the brain, keeping it healthy. Chemicals such as dopamine and serotonin are released during exercise giving a sensation of wellbeing. Young children and teenagers are frequently sleep deprived which severely affects mood and the brains capacity to learn.

We recommend that parents and teachers consider whether adjustments need to be made in children's lifestyle to ensure that they have adequate nourishing food, regular exercise, times for reflection and the appropriate amount of sleep. We have heard of schools that have cut down on the number and length of break times to increase time allocated to the formal curriculum, without considering the unintended consequences. These include reducing time to develop social and interpersonal skills. We have been pleased to see though that early years settings are reintroducing nap times for children.

Activity 1: Understanding the basic structure of our brains

There is a simple hand model that you can use with pupils to help them gain an understanding of the brain. We find that it grabs their attention and aids memory. Adapt the following text to suit the age and stage of your pupils.

Hold up your left arm and tell your pupils that you are going to create a basic model of the human brain using your arm and hand. Invite them to use their imagination and to hold up their left arm so that their hand is no higher than eye level.

Demonstrate with your own left arm, pointing with your right hand to your forearm, which represents the spinal column that comes up the centre of our back. Now point to the base of your hand, just above the wrist, and explain that this area represents the brain stem. Sometimes this is referred to as the reptilian brain, as in evolutionary terms it was the first part of the brain to evolve and is found in reptiles. The brain stem is involved in the control of basic body functions such as breathing, swallowing, heart rate, blood pressure and body temperature.

Next ask the pupils to place their thumb across the palm, fingers extended. The thumb represents the limbic area of the brain. The limbic area emerged in the first mammals. It is associated with our emotions and records memories of behaviours that produce agreeable and disagreeable experiences. The main structures of the human limbic system are the hippocampus, (mainly associated with memory), the amygdala (associated with survival instincts such as fear and other emotions) and the hypothalamus (this controls body temperature, hunger and important aspects of parenting and attachment behaviours). The limbic part of the brain is the seat of value judgements that we make, often unconsciously, that exert such a strong influence on our behaviour. Incidentally, we think that this is a powerful reason for introducing VbE, because it helps to strengthen the conscious part of our brain, which can think about and adopt values that are beneficial to the individual and humanity in general.

Finally, ask your pupils to close their fingers over their thumb and tilt the hand slightly forward. The fingers represent the cortex that engulfs the limbic system and connects to the brain stem. We are especially interested in the section that is represented by the second fingers joints. This area, often referred to as the executive function of the brain, is the middle prefrontal cortex – PFC for short. This part of the brain is the seat of complex cognitive behaviour, personality expression, decision-making, and moderating social behaviour.

Now you can demonstrate to the pupils what happens when we are overwhelmed by the emotions produced by our limbic system. When we feel a very strong emotion, such as anger, we can 'flip our lid'. When you say this, quickly detach your fingers from your thumb, revealing your thumb. This action represents how, when we are subjected to strong emotion, the functions of the prefrontal cortex are disconnected from the limbic system and emotions can reign supreme. As the system calms down the prefrontal cortex reconnects with the limbic system and the brain stem. Again show this process as the fingers close over the thumb.

Benefits

When you work with this simple model you will soon appreciate that knowledge about how our brain works brings a greater self-awareness to your pupils. It is remarkable that, by having this information, pupils begin to understand what is happening to them when they are upset and they can look to calm themselves. A boy in a London school, who had been in an emotional state, told his headteacher that he was sorry for his behaviour: his excuse was that he was having an amygdala hijack! The school teaches a program about the brain called 'Mind Up'.

Activity 2: The plastic water bottle

Jane loves demonstrating this next activity, both to children and adults. It is especially popular in primary classrooms. Its purpose is to represent what happens to us when we flip our lids and feel upset. Often this happens during break times when children are in free play situations. Pupils often request to hold the bottle!

Find a large clear plastic bottle, add some glitter and fill with water and seal it. You may like to make a more sophisticated version by adding plastic values letters and some glycerine or similar substance, which slows down the rate of settlement. Carry out a test before showing your pupils, to make sure that after shaking up the bottle the contents will slowly settle. The whirling glitter represents how we feel when we are upset; we feel all shaken up and disturbed. Ask the pupils to give you examples, which they are willing to talk about, of times when they have felt upset. Get one of them to hold and shake up the bottle whilst everyone watches as the glitter settles. Explain to them why they have these feelings; you can, perhaps, refer to the previous exercise to help explain the process of getting upset.

In a Herefordshire school at break time, a group of Year 3 children came into the classroom in which we were working. The children were curious about our glitter bottle. After Jane explained about it to the group one of the boys who had been listening said: 'Ah, that's just like me, sometimes I am as good as gold, like the glitter, I feel settled. But sometimes I feel so upset I want to run out of the class, because I am like the bottle when it is shaken'. He paused and said, 'I would like a bottle like that'.

The bottle or several of them can be stored in the class and when pupils feel upset they can shake one and watch it settle, whilst experiencing how their own mood calms down.

Benefits

Many teachers have told us that this simple tool has helped maintain a peaceful atmosphere in their class and cut down the time spent listening to complaints about behaviour at break times. It seems that when we calm down, our natural healing energy is allowed to come into our system and what we saw as a huge issue doesn't have the same impact. We are not implying that serious incidents should not be dealt with in other more structured ways. Try using such a bottle with your pupils and see what happens.

Activity 3: Brain breaks

The next exercise we would like to introduce to you is one we find is so simple to do, yet is so profound in its effects. This is a technique that we have known by many names such as traffic control – slowing down the traffic of the mind, or, 'pausing to be', which we will delve into in more depth later.

Brain breaks literally do that; they give the brain a break from its work, allowing, through stillness and calmness, clarity to emerge.

You will need a chime bar for this exercise. You should practice with your class so that they will know that when they hear the chime bar it is a time to pause, be still and quiet.

Let us give you an example. An active science lesson is in progress and you sense that your pupils are losing focus and the atmosphere is beginning to bubble. Without saying anything you strike the chime bar and stand or sit still, modelling what you want the pupils to do. In turn the pupils close their eyes and in silence go inward to their internal worlds. They know that this is a time just to be and observe what's happening to them internally. As the moments go by the thoughts in their minds appear to slow down and their mood is calmer. When you sense that it is time, perhaps a minute or two has gone by, then again strike the chime bar. This is the signal to pupils that they continue with the activity in which they were engaged. What you will find is that the students are now more focused on the activity.

Jane was talking about brain breaks to a large group of pupils in Luton that were assembled for an inter-schools values' day. One of the younger children, from a Year 1 class, put her hand up wanting to share her experience and said: 'When my teacher hits the chime bar, then we pause and we let all our thinking go from our brain'. She showed this by using her two hands moving gently apart across her forehead. She continued: 'So our brains are then ready for their new learning'.

A variation of this method includes, after striking the chime bar, asking the pupils to pause, take their attention to their internal world, and review what they are trying to achieve in the activity and how they can get the most from it. This adds a reflective dimension to brain breaks, which again has beneficial effects on learning. We invite you to experiment with your own variations of this exercise and ask the pupils to suggest other ways that the technique can be used.

Benefits

This reflective technique helps to strengthen the executive parts of the brain, which gives the pupil greater awareness about their mental processes. We will be explaining more about the benefits of stillness and reflection in a later section. We think you will gain a more comprehensive insight into what we are suggesting in the next section, which looks at the science of interpersonal neurobiology.

Going a bit deeper

As we outlined, we think pupils should have an understanding of the structure of the human brain so that they understand how the different parts influence their thinking and behaviour. Such an understanding strengthens their ability to work on that part of the Inner Curriculum, which is about recognising that they can positively influence the state of their mind. The intention is to give them greater self-control and maintain a sense of wellbeing. You may be wondering how this happens.

Dr. Dan Sigel describes in a personal, real life story how a mute child was brought to his surgery for treatment. He soon discovered that the child's mum had been in a bad car accident and had not been wearing a safety belt. She had severely damaged the part of her brain just behind her forehead, when her head hit the steering wheel, which is called the middle prefrontal cortex. Dan learned that the mum used to be a bright, happy person who enthusiastically interacted with her children, but after the accident her relational skills were impaired. The daughter was devastated because of her mother's change in mood and behaviour. This trauma prevented the child from talking. The mum told Dan that it was as though she had lost her soul after the accident – her real self.

This case led to Dan researching what the PFC does and how it interrelates with the activity of the limbic system (the source of feelings and emotions) beneath it. Dan's work has two main conclusions: firstly, the PFC is like a control centre that has nine main functions with specific outcomes and that are crucial for pro-social behaviour. The first seven functions are also associated with good parent-child attachment, i.e. children who have parents to whom they feel securely attached develop these seven capacities. Secondly, Dan's research led to his assertion that we can shape our brains to strengthen the beneficial functions of the PFC, this outcome being achieved through a process of mindful awareness practice. You may recognize that Dan's nine outcomes are also significant outcomes of VbE.

Dan's work is showing how our brains are hardwired to connect with others and build relationships. Therefore, we can use our intention to strengthen our brains in particular ways and trigger them for better health. It is literally self-liberating. The result is that we have a deeper sense of wellbeing and form better relationships.

What does Dan Siegel's work suggest that our brain's middle prefrontal cortex does? What are its incredible nine functions that we benefit from nourishing?

1. The PFC affects **body regulation** by overriding the limbic system and brain stem when necessary. This means that it can take control of our autonomic nervous system, which regulates our heartbeat and breathing. It is connected to our nervous system and acts as an accelerator or break would do in a car, either revving us up for action of calming us down.

2. It promotes **attuned communication**. Attunement is at the core of successful human relationships because through it we recognise the verbal and non-verbal signals of others and are able to respond appropriately. Resonating to another, by tuning into them, alters our physiological state and makes us feel close to that person. When another person feels this feeling we feel safe, which is at the heart of wellbeing.

3. The PFC influences **emotional balance** by regulating our emotions. The limbic areas of the brain generate affective states such as sadness, joy, anger and excitement. The PFC monitors and influences such sub cortical (below the cortex) areas of the brain.

4. **Response flexibility** is another function of the PFC. This function gives us the ability to pause, creating the opportunity to determine appropriate actions. The PFC creates a space between stimulus and response, strengthening emotional and social intelligence.

5. **Insight** is the capacity of minds to create mental time travel, connecting the past with present and future. It helps us to create a coherent narrative, so that we are the active authors of our own lives. Insight gives us self-knowing awareness, allowing us to modify our character traits. Parents who have this capacity are more likely to form secure attachments with their child. Mindful awareness enhances insight. A key indicator of a child's ability to develop secure attachments and thrive in school is the degree to which the parent(s) has self-understanding gained through insight.

6. **Empathy** is the next outcome of having a healthy prefrontal cortex. Empathy helps us to understand another's point-of-view and generates

compassion. Dan has coined the term 'mindsight', a combination of insight and empathy, which is the ability to sense what's going on in the mind of another and to see the world through another's perspective.

7. **Fear modulation**. Simply described, the PFC can calm down the responses of the amygdala, a part of our limbic system, which creates the sensation of fear. We modulate the fear response through activities such as reflection/mindfulness, which stimulates the growth of new neurons from the PFC.

8. **Being in touch with intuition**. This is the process of the PFC in which it is open to the intuitive wisdom of the body, through a system of neurons around our organs such as the heart and intestines.

9. **Morality**. Incredibly, Dan found that without the PFC we struggle to see life through a moral perspective. Morality, he defines as thinking about the greater social good, having feelings of a deep sense of compassion for others. The PFC is essential so that we can be aware of the greater social good.

Dan's list of the nine functions of the PFC makes it crystal clear why the Inner Curriculum is so very important in education. We describe it as 'the work before the work'. That is, children will be more successful learners if they have paid attention to developing these nine aspects of the PFC. Also, it is important for adults to remember that it is the way that we treat children which will affect the healthy growth of the PFC brain fibres that create the capacity for self-regulation. A key method to cultivate this capacity is through mindful awareness, which is activated through activities such as reflection/mindfulness. An outcome is the capacity of self-attunement, realising that you are your own best friend, which leads to the ability to attune with others. As neurons in the PFC fire and wire together they literally increase the size of the PFC, a possible reason why meditators have thicker PFCs.

Now that you have a useful general understanding of the human brain, let us go on and explore the second key aspect of the Inner Curriculum, which is a range of experiences under the general heading of reflective practices that we believe should be thought of as the fourth 'R' in education.

Chapter 4:
Exploring reflective practices

'To meet everything and everyone through stillness instead of mental noise is the greatest gift you can offer the universe.'

– Eckhart Tolle

As we learn about the structure and functions of our brains we can then begin to build an understanding of how we access our internal world and discover the secrets of the Inner Curriculum.

Is there a method that enables us to sense our true self and find the gifts that it contains? Through our own reflective practice we have sensed and grown our ability to be self-led. This means that we are less likely to be controlled by any random thought or emotion, but remain in a peaceful stillness that helps us to be authentic. We have achieved this through the daily reflective practice of going inward in periods of silent sitting for 30 minutes. We do not wish to imply that we have mastered the technique, as we are aware that we are on a journey of self-empowerment, which we invite you to join.

Neil taught, and we both still do, the rudiments of this work to pupils and adults as a headteacher, calling it 'pause to be'. Neil discovered that self-leadership and agency was the outcome, which is the ability of pupils to take greater responsibility for their learning and behaviour.

The practice of reflection, which is also called silent sitting, mindfulness or meditation, occurs when we pause and focus our attention inside ourselves. Space and time is needed for this practice to grow, embed and its effects felt. Sometimes we find that adults are reticent or feel self-conscious to explore the potential of reflective practice. However teachers and others tell us that once they have experienced the benefits of reflection for themselves then they are more likely to introduce it to pupils. Such a teacher is Jasmine Cross who, before moving to teach in New Zealand, was a values-based teacher at Poynton High School in the UK. Jasmine told us:

'I have found reflection so personally empowering. I couldn't wait to form a reflection/mindfulness group at school as I think secondary school students really need the support that it gives.'

'I have had so much positive feedback from students. One of them said, 'I really look forward to mindfulness – especially as it is mid-week and it helps me reflect and de-stress. It creates a new perspective on anything that might have happened prior to it, and anything that might happen after it.' Another student commented, 'I always feel so calm after the reflection sessions – the deep sense of peace stays and a sense of strength as well.'

'Another student said, 'I just find that every time I feel overwhelmed or stressed with school work and exams, if I go home to my room, light some candles, play some calming music and lie on my bed and just breathe everything seems to melt away.'

'One of my students was suffering from anxiety and wasn't attending lessons but through the mindfulness group and by practicing at home was transformed and was now able to go back into lessons and cope with school life.'

We hope that you have been inspired by Jasmine's account. The beginning point for reflective practice is being consciously aware of your breath.

Breathing

May we invite you to pause in your reading and take a minute to be aware of your breathing?

What did you experience?

Most of the time we are not conscious about our breathing, as it is automatic and with us throughout life. When we asked you to be aware of your breathing you may have stopped breathing in a shallow, rhythmical way, becoming self-conscious, disturbing the rhythm of your breathing process. However, we are convinced that by regularly practicing this simple technique it will bring many benefits to you, such as increased concentration, pausing to think before taking actions, emotional regulation, such as feeling calmer; appreciating that a thought is just a thought and we can choose our thoughts. For instance, if you sense that your thoughts are becoming critical of someone then you can change them to being curious.

Jane has worked with numerous groups of adults and children to help them to understand these truths. Typically, Jane invites a group to sit with dignity, either closing their eyes or keeping them open so that their gaze rests on something. She then invites them to focus their attention on their breathing. She explains that when they realise that they are no longer focusing on their breathing, then they are to gently redirect their awareness back to their breath.

This practice strengthens the neural pathways of the brain and is a key skill to learn in the practice of mindfulness, which is the ability to deliberately direct your attention in moment-to-moment, non-judgemental awareness.

We have watched very young pupils at a kindergarten in Iceland lie on their backs whilst a teacher placed a small toy on each of their stomachs. The challenge was to breathe more deeply with the stomach rising and falling with each breath, but ensuring that the toy stayed resting where it was placed. This fun activity helped the children to remain conscious of their breathing whilst a physical process was taking place. Taking time to increase the depth of our breathing has the physical benefit of increasing the level of oxygen in the blood. If we are emotionally upset then by taking a few deep breaths we can feel calmer.

The practice of focusing on the breath sounds so simple but it is difficult to maintain and is a great exercise with which to begin a lesson on visualisation.

Visualisation

Visualisation is an effective reflective method to encourage the imagination to sense our inner world, using its healing energy to empower us to be authentically ourselves.

We invite you to understand and then practice a visualisation that we have called 'The Wisdom Star'. We have seen that this reflective, creative work has transformational qualities that can enhance your life and those whom you encourage to use it.

Introduction to The Wisdom Star

We are aware that what we outline below needs to be adapted to the age and stage of pupils so that they can understand the concept of the Wisdom Star. In our experience some pupils will quickly and readily enjoy working with the ideas, whilst others may be more reticent. As with all our exercises it is important that you are comfortable with it before sharing it with others.

Let us imagine that each of us is born with a very special gift. The gift is precious and is available for everyone to use on a regular basis or when life needs some help or support.

This special gift may be visualised, seen, as our very own Wisdom Star. We may see it radiating a special helping healing energy to us, which we can access anytime we need it. This energy, which comes from the core of our star, is really the essence of who we are – our authentic true Self.

We receive help from our star when sitting quietly, closing our eyes and seeing, visualising or sensing, our wisdom star. We are mindful that some people may find it difficult to visualise a star, some may never – be patient. What colour is your star? What shape is it? What size does it appear to be? As we concentrate on seeing our own wisdom star, its innate energy helps us to be wise and kind for the benefit of others and our self.

To access our star's dynamic energy so that it can help us with a problem or situation we are worried about, we use what we call the *wisdom cycle*, which is a simple yet profound way to bring our positive values to act as a compass to guide our thoughts and actions.

This is how we do it: we pause, sit still and as we visualise our wisdom star we think of a situation in our lives for which we need our wisdom star's help. Perhaps we could do with some help with our relationships, or we want to draw on our Star's wisdom to help us make a good decision. For instance, if we feel overwhelmed with anger we can visualise our star and receive from it the value of peace. By using this value we self-sooth and calm ourselves. Or, we may feel sad and need our star's gift of compassion. Our star has many values that help us to face life's challenges positively. Here are some of your star's values – they are eight values we all share – you may think of others: calmness, curiosity, compassion, courage, confidence, clarity, creativity and connectedness.

Our Wisdom Star helps us to develop what we call 'values powers', which grow in us as we live the values shared with us by our wisdom star.

Our Wisdom Star helps us to develop these values powers (virtues):

- The power to pause.
- The power to love.
- The power to be wise.
- The power to be compassionate.
- The power to be altruistic.
- The power to experience wellbeing.
- The power to be peaceful.
- The power to be resilient.
- The power to connect with others.
- The power to be self-led.

It is through the process of deliberately and consistently accessing our Wisdom Star that we grow into being a humane, reflective person who creates the transformational sustainable conditions that our world so urgently needs.

Visualisation exercise: The Wisdom Star

Now let us give time to experiencing the Wisdom Star in a visualisation. It is a visualisation to practice on a regular basis. We recommend that you experience the visualisation in a quiet, still space, uninterrupted by distractions. Ideally someone will read it too you, pausing where indicated (...). This visualisation we recommend for people who are more than seven years old. If you are using it with younger children then please feel free to adapt it to the age and stage of the pupils.

Introduction

Please be aware that the screen of your mind can be likened to a television set or a cinema screen. Don't be concerned if you can't create a picture on it because it takes practice for most; for some it is difficult, and for a few impossible, so just begin by allowing yourself to have an awareness of your star.

We recommend that at the end of the visualisation with children you invite them to draw their star labelling it with its values (qualities). Also we recommend that the children keep a Wisdom Star Journal so that they can write about their values, what they mean and the experiences they are having with them. Your inner creativity will grow the more you practice and access this faculty.

The Visualisation

Sitting comfortably and with dignity, close your eyes and give your attention to your breathing. Focus on your breathing. As you breathe out, feel the sensation of your breath leaving your body.

If your mind wanders and thinks of other things, which is quite normal, then gently return the focus of your attention to your breath. As you become aware of your wandering mind and refocus on your breath you are developing the skill of awareness.

For the next minute focus on your breathing with an awareness of peacefulness...

(In the early stages of practicing this exercise some find it helpful to focus if they say 'in' and 'out' in their minds as they breathe.)

Now visualise a beautiful, radiant shining star; see its colours and its shape. You can see that it has lots of pulsating star-likepoints emerging from its core... what you are seeing is your Wisdom Star, which contains many values that are nourishing gifts to support you in your life. Your star is accessible to you whenever you need one of its gifts...

Now take a moment to sense what value would help you on your life's journey today. See the value pulsating calmly towards you on a beam of light, and the essence of you feeling its presence...merge yourself in this value, feeling it's sublime qualities.

Which value did you chose? Name your value and sense by naming it the powerful energy that it gives to you.

For the next few moments take the time and space to experience your star's gift as energising sensations that will support you today and into the future...

Now gently, and in your own time, return your attention to the awareness of this room and the people within it.

During this exercise you will have created a special peaceful atmosphere. So if you are working with pupils allow a few quiet moments to bring this special quality into their awareness. The atmosphere may be sustained as you invite them to engage with some creative follow-up in their Wisdom Star journal.

Conclusion

We hope you have been inspired to consider other reflective practice exercises. Neil enjoyed leading pupils to explore reflective practices during lesson and assembly times. We are convinced that with regular practice children learn to access and self-regulate their inner worlds, empowering their self-energy, which helps them to live more authentically and compassionately.

There are many resources that can be found on the web to build on the basic ideas we have shared with you. We particularly recommend for younger children the *Relax Kids* materials, for older pupils *dot b (.b)* and *Mindup* for all ages and for adults the works of Jon Kabat-Zinn, Tich Nhat Hanh and Jack Kornfield.

Our next section will give you a number of other useful tools that will help you and the children you support flourish in the world.

Chapter 5:
The Internal Family System (IFS): helping us understand our internal world

'Self is in everybody; it is our birthright. It doesn't need to be developed, it can't be damaged, and it knows how to heal both internally and externally, but is covered over by protective parts.'

– Richard Schwartz

The model of VbE is based on our understanding that positive human values such as peace, love, trust and resilience can be introduced to children acting as their compass in life to guide their thinking and behaviour. VbE recognises that we all begin life with limitless potential. However, its realisation will depend on how we build on the positive sides of human nature and are given care and love by our parents, caregivers, educators and community.

Historically, some ways of thinking about people have focused on our flaws, which have in some cases led to harsh punitive methods of control, such as the corporal punishment of children. Also, some thinking contained in academic disciplines, such as developmental psychology, have argued that our basic nature is dependent on the kind of parenting we receive. That if we have any valuable qualities then they are pumped into us from the outside world. It is our experience that aspects of the education system seem dominated by variations of such a shortfall view of human nature, which we think limits children's potential.

In contrast, VbE and the Inner Curriculum do not pathologise, as they do not examine what may be wrong with people and how this can be fixed. Neither do they argue that morality should be imposed on children by coercion or fear. Such views have led us to consider how we can best support children and young people to develop positive character traits that will benefit them and society?

Traditionally in schools we are taught to look outside of ourselves to understand the world and ourselves but we think we should begin by looking inside ourselves first.

If this claim is valid, then is there a method that will help us learn about and understand our internal world? We are aware that there are a number of helpful models, but we think that there is one that resonates most clearly with the principles of VbE and our understanding of interpersonal neurobiology. This method is called the Internal Family System or IFS.

We are aware that in this chapter we are deliberately giving you a full and comprehensive account of IFS. We are also indebted to Dr. Ralph Cohen who has contributed to the wording and structure of this chapter. Our aim is that you will be inspired to want to delve into IFS theory and practices. We recommend that before you try to implement IFS that you attend one of our workshops or one offered by the Centre for Self Leadership.

We first met Richard (Dick) Schwartz, founder of the Internal Family System in Iceland at an international conference – a profound moment of synchronicity. We felt humbled by the array of transformational speakers who had been assembled to consider how the spirit of humanity could be lifted to help the sustainability of our world.

For ten years we had been considering what it is that makes VbE so impactful. We had realised that VbE contained the rudiments of what we described as an Inner Curriculum, which empowered both adults and pupils to flourish both academically and as people. Jane became acutely aware that in VbE schools there was an 'X' factor, an energy that created harmony, connection, agency, trust, resilience and wellbeing. We believed that the experiential nature of living the values words of VbE, in the context of good relationships, created this energy, but what is the energy?

We discovered the answer in Iceland when Jane experienced the power of self-energy during an IFS therapeutic session with Dick. Neil, too, exchanged insights of VbE and IFS with Dick and we realised that we had stumbled on the secret power of VbE – self-energy and in what circumstances, and how, it is activated.

Jane has subsequently received the full IFS training from Dick and his colleagues as an IFS therapist: level one and two in the UK, and level three in Seattle in the USA. At the time of writing this book, Neil is engaged in the process of being trained as an IFS practitioner. Prior to this, Neil had been a part of Jane's IFS journey, deepening his understanding of the theory as he had taken every opportunity to discuss with her, as well as face-to face or through media links with Dick, the connections between the models of VbE and IFS. Our conclusion is that for education and humanity to flourish, we all need to understand that character development, wellbeing, resilience and achievement are directly linked to the level of self-energy within the personal or organisational system. Until recently VbE schools have implicitly developed this energy but now they will, through an understanding of the Inner Curriculum and IFS, be able to make it explicit. Furthermore, we think that teachers and support staff need to be given the understanding that IFS provides, so that they can build with confidence on their practical experience of working with pupils.

What is contained in the IFS model?

The Internal Family System is a guide to our internal world and how to nourish the capacity of self-leadership.

All of us are complex people that are capable of a wide-range of beliefs, emotions and patterns of behaviour. As humans, we are able to observe our thoughts, feelings and actions; making decisions about how to organise our experiences. At times, each of us experiences conflicting reactions and understandings to situations inside ourselves, sometimes feeling confused, ambivalent or even frozen. During these times, we usually have the capacity to step back, consider all sides of our inner arguments, and come to a reasonable decision. We call the phenomenon of having many autonomous minds 'multiplicity', a normal and natural characteristic of being human.

In day-to-day language, people speak about different 'parts' of themselves as holding different attitudes, emotions, and reactions to life experiences. These parts can be thought of as our internal people of different ages, talents and temperaments, each with their own story and role in our internal system. Parts can be experienced as: thoughts, feelings, sensations, images, words, sounds, inner voices and physical symptoms. A core tenant of IFS is that all parts are welcome!

What is the nature of our 'parts'?

Our parts are with us at birth and materialise as we develop. They show themselves in our bodies, as we can often feel or sense when our parts are present. For instance, we are aware of our parts when we are nervous and experience butterflies in our stomachs, when sad we feel a sense of heaviness, and when angry we may experience a sensation of 'seeing red' and numbness. Current research using Functional MRI is able to show through brain measurements differences in how the neurons in our brains fire when we are experiencing our different parts or when we are in a state of self-leadership.

What is the 'self'?

The 'you' who can observe and communicate with our parts is referred to as the 'self'. The self, which can be thought of as the 'essence' of who we are, is an innate healing energy that is nurtured in relationship and connects us to each other. It is also considered to be the 'seat of consciousness' – it is the 'I' that observes and interacts internally with our parts and relates to the self and parts of others in effective ways.

The self contains the qualities of self-leadership, known in IFS as the '8 C's of Self-Leadership': calmness, compassion, curiosity, clarity, courage, confidence, creativity and connectedness. We all have a self that is capable of providing leadership to our parts and to others in a compassionate and non-judging way. However, the self is sometimes obscured by some of our parts that, for one reason or another, do not accept the leadership of the self and feel that they need to take extreme actions to feel safe and secure.

The self-led system: the relationship of self and parts

A useful metaphor highlighting the relationship of the self and our parts is that of a beloved orchestra conductor. While the conductor does not play an instrument in the orchestra, he knows the music in detail and interprets the intentions of the composer to create an integrated whole. He understands the nature of each instrument and knows his musicians well. His musicians know and trust the conductor to cue them at the proper moments and to bring out the best in each musician. He is able to relate to each member of the orchestra as a unique individual, responding to the needs of all in a non-judging and compassionate manner. He is able to relate to the audience to create a pleasurable experience through the positive relationships he has cultivated with the musicians.

In summary, the conductor represents the 8 C's of Self-Leadership, creating both balance and harmony in the orchestra with such leadership.

This is an example of a healthy system; when applied within a person, the self operates in the role of the orchestra conductor, supplying one's parts with a sense of unity and connection to the whole, accessing the various resources of one's parts for the good of all.

Let's now consider an inner system that is not as healthy, what IFS calls a 'dysregulated' system.

The dysregulated inner system

In a perfect world, each of us would be living our lives in a self-led manner and our parts would be in balance and harmony. While this would certainly be an ideal, we are often thrown out of balance and operate in polarised and self-protective ways – often to the detriment of others and ourselves. How do our internal systems become dysregulated?

As children, in order to learn to trust our own self, we need to have connection with people who look after us – caretakers who can help us to feel nurtured, safe and valued. This requires that adults who are charged with our wellbeing to have at least, what Dick Schwartz calls a 'critical mass of self-energy in their system'. Though sometimes as children our needs are frustrated, we come to learn that we ultimately rely on our caregivers to take care of us and love us. Through the eyes and actions of our caretakers, we receive feedback that we are valued, loved and worthy.

In our imperfect worlds, however, we often receive mixed messages as children and learn that our caretakers and family members place conditional worth on us – that we must behave in certain ways, believe in certain things, and conform to expectations about our gender, culture, social standing, and so forth. When we are faced with such demands, we 'exile' those parts of us that do not conform, or risk devaluation, abandonment, and withdrawal of love. In consequence we adopt behaviours, beliefs and rules that prevent us from suffering the effects of being different from what is expected of us.

Also, when we face traumatising situations, parts of us absorb the painful memories, emotions, sensations, beliefs about our security and pain of our experiences – what IFS therapists call 'burdens'. These are ideas and beliefs that are formed at the time of experiences that have a significant impact on the system and become attached to one of the parts. Often they are limiting beliefs about the person, and associated with shame. Especially when we are very young and unable to protect or defend ourselves, we are particularly vulnerable to being hurt. As young children, we naturally want to trust others and learn about the world. Children who are exposed to domestic violence, bullied in school, witness harm or devaluing comments made toward others, or are violated themselves (physically, emotionally or sexually) tend to absorb the burdens and hold them inside. These parts want to release the burdens and restore connection with their caretakers and will develop strategies to attempt to get their needs met. This can often lead to further exposure to those who hurt them in the first place, or to being victimised by a family or school system that doesn't account for the trauma that the child has suffered. Please note that any life event, such as the loss of a parent, can cause trauma; it can become a burden if it is not talked about and integrated into the internal system.

In these instances, other parts of us take on the role of exiling parts of ourselves that carry burdens and our internal systems develop extreme measures to keep these parts hidden or safe. In such devaluing or traumatising situations, we become overwhelmed, feel alone and are left to fend for ourselves. We don't have access to our own self or the self-energy of those who should be protecting and validating our experiences. Instead, we feel shamed, vulnerable, unlovable, needy, and worthless. These feelings further make us vulnerable to criticism, attack, and devaluation from others.

In the absence of trust in the self, parts of us are forced into extreme protective roles, where survival is the primary objective and takes precedence over values-based ways of being. Consequently, a dysregulated system is activated that, in the absence of self-leadership, some parts take on the role of 'protectors'. Other parts are forced into the role of 'exiles', which are both in need of protection and viewed by some protectors as threats to the system that need to be controlled or destroyed.

Some parts are called 'managers', as their roles are to run the internal system in ways to protect exiles or keep us away from the burdens that exiles carry. As stated above, exiles are the parts of us that have been isolated within our system because they have been hurt and carry unresolved painful memories and experiences. Parts are sometimes forced into manager roles, which may be seen to be counter-productive, but they believe that our survival depends on the roles they play.

Managers constantly scan the environment for potential dangers that would expose exiles. They work overtime to ensure that the world is safe and predictable. Examples of characteristic roles that parts adopt as managers include: controlling, judging, critical of others, extreme caretaking, perfectionism, critical of oneself, and other means of controlling the environment or other people.

Other protector parts are called 'firefighters'. Like managers, their role is to protect the system from the burdens that exiles carry, but react when the managers are unable to keep exiles at bay. These parts are often associated with more extreme behaviours, e.g. addictions, self-harming, using unnecessary work as a distraction, or any behaviour that is developed to stop the pain of an exile from being felt. They go into action when they think the manager role is not protecting the exile and jump in with their ways of protection.

Exiles, managers and firefighters often take on their roles during our early childhood development, and throughout our life in response to life's events, that are unresolved. They frequently become stuck at the age of the unresolved incident/trauma, and are truly amazed to find out how old the person might now be.

In the absence of self-leadership, these various protectors (both managers and firefighters) vie for control and often polarise against each other to claim power and control. Once these parts take over in their extreme roles, it is very difficult to get them to shift back to their more preferred, non-extreme roles for fear that the system will be overcome by the burdens carried by exiles and that we will be vulnerable to being hurt further.

From dysregulation to being self-led: restoring leadership, balance and harmony

What is the answer to helping our parts to be free from burdens and being able to restore balance and harmony in our internal systems?

Before answering this question, there is analogy that you may find helpful. When someone breaks a leg, the doctors do not heal the leg. Instead, they put it in a cast to allow the body to heal itself. In the same way, teachers do not become responsible for healing their students' minds. Their bodies are equipped to do it for themselves. Instead, we create an environment that is the equivalent of a plaster cast, providing the right conditions for self-healing to take place. It is very important to note that our suggested exercises and tools are not appropriate for children or adults with mental illnesses, or with traumas that are so severe that professional help is required.

First, we must work with our protectors to re-introduce the self back into the system, re-establishing trust in the self. Secondly, in gaining more trust in the self, we must get permission from our protectors to work with exiles without their interference. Thirdly, once we are able to establish a compassionate and self-led connection with the exiled parts, we can help them to release their burdens through a process of being witnessed by the self.

This healing relationship between the self and exiled parts allows the release of the exiles' burdens, thus removing the threat to the system. The parts that were protecting the system from these burdens can shift out of their extreme protective roles and take on new roles that are free from fear and anxiety. With a new connection to the self, parts can realign their relationships with each other and to the self and parts of others in non-extreme ways with a restored sense of balance and harmony in the system.

A key to understanding the model is to appreciate that 'all parts are welcome'. This means that every part has a positive intention, even if the thinking and behaviour of a part maybe seen to be unhelpful. When the self focuses on them with its innate non-judging, curious and openhearted perspective, their stories can be deeply understood. This then opens up the possibility for unburdening, letting go of former limiting beliefs, and the opportunity to invite new qualities, into the part, and a new role within the system.

If our lives are predominately parts led, then our innate self-energy is obscured. We believe that a key outcome of VbE is the manifestation of self-energy, as the adults and children find the safety to relax, their manager parts feeling understood and appreciated. As more self-energy comes in to each individual person's system, more is manifest in the school, which create the conditions for effective learning and teaching.

As parts relax our system opens up to self-energy, with its innate qualities of: curiosity, compassion, calmness, courage, confidence, clarity, creativity and connectedness, the 8 C's of Self-Leadership and what we recognise in VbE as the values of self-leadership. As parts trust the self to lead our system we experience more of these innate values.

The critical role of self-led adults in the lives of children

With an IFS set of lenses, we can understand the role of adults in the development of self-leadership and values-based processes in children.

With an awareness of the neurobiology of brain development and mirror neurons, we understand the power of modelling of self-leadership in children's brain development. It also teaches us the importance of creating a safe environment for secure attachment and supporting and anchoring self-esteem in children (i.e. the awareness of having a 'self'). In order for adults to provide these resources for healthy development of our children's internal systems, we must learn about our own internal worlds and strive to work on our own dysregulation by connecting with our own self-leadership. This requires that we must first 'put the oxygen mask on ourselves' by creating communities that supports values-based relationships for all.

We will now share with you some practical ways of working with the IFS model.

IFS and Values-based Education

VbE and the Inner Curriculum empower self so that it can transform values into a person's virtues, otherwise known as positive character traits. It seems to us that what stop values from being as transformational as they might be is that our life experiences, as explained above, and often a rigid mindset or worldview stops us embracing them. In other words, parts that have been burdened or exiled prevent the healing that comes from embracing a value, such as respect or tolerance.

We think that the following quote from Albert Einstein helps us to see the bigger picture and the relevance of IFS and VbE, as they widen our circles of compassion:

'A human being is part of a whole, called by us the 'universe', a part limited in time and space. He experiences himself, his thoughts and feelings, as something separated from the rest – a kind of optical delusion of his consciousness. This delusion is a kind of prison for us, restricting us to our personal desires and to affection for a few persons near to us. Our task must be to free ourselves from this prison by widening our circles of compassion to embrace all living creatures and the whole of nature in its beauty.'

Over the decades that Jane has worked as a psychotherapist, she has heard many real life stories about how adults in their significant roles of parents, grandparents and teachers have been both phenomenal mentors and carers to vulnerable children whilst others, in the same roles, have left children with very low self-esteem and a sense of being unlovable. If children have had the latter experience their systems are more likely to be run by controlling, powerful manager and firefighter parts. These parts will be protecting the vulnerable exiles and even though their life chances will now be very different, the young parts continue to see the world as a dangerous place and that people are not to be trusted. However, if consistent kind adults come alongside a child that has had trauma then the events of the trauma are decoded and the child's self-energy is released to heal.

So how do we support everyone to be self-led?

Firstly by becoming aware of our internal world and building relationship with our own parts! Remember 'all parts are welcome!' It is natural that some parts will have strong feelings about other parts. Just as you would with any method of conflict resolution, you learn to support your parts to understand why they believe what they do, and especially listen to the fears each will have as to what might happen if they changed. Just spending time every day with your internal world will start you on a life practice that will sustain you and nourish your innate self-energy.

Taking time to be with any part that is struggling, or maybe overwhelming the system, will give you a great insight into the story you have created about yourself. It will give you the opportunity to release painful memories and beliefs and take on new qualities to transform your story and your life.

Exercises and case studies

Health warning: May we remind you that before doing any work with children that it's important that you have worked on yourself experiencing this new way of understanding yourself, and ideally had opportunities to discuss and work with another colleague. Maybe you will attend an introductory course in IFS, or have some in-service training for your whole school. It is not our intention to give the impression that having this knowledge you are qualified to be an IFS therapist. If you would like training in IFS then please contact Jane Hawkes at www.valuesbasededucation.com and/or look on the IFS website for more information www.internalfamilysystemstraining.co.uk.

However we think that you will be able to use and share relevant concepts with pupils. From our own observations we think aspects of IFS are appropriate for children of all ages – appropriate to age and stage of development. Secondary school aged pupils will be able to grasp the concepts and we think gain much by understanding and applying them.

We hope that by developing an understanding of IFS through the following exercises, pupils will be on a journey that will help them to:

- Achieve harmony and balance in their internal world.

- Understand that a part of them may be behaving in a particular way, but this is not the whole of them.

- Know that all parts are welcome.

- Appreciate that they have parts of them that behave in certain ways.

- Parts are often younger aspects of us and act from the age we were when the part was developed – they often think we are younger than we are.

- Know that all parts are valuable and, if asked, will let you know what their positive intention is.

- Understand why and how these parts developed in their system.

- Develop a positive identity based on an understanding of self.

- Acquire the ability to lead from self not from parts.

- Know and experience how to nourish and use the healing energy of self through reflective practices.

- Be aware that others may be parts driven and have compassion for them.

- Be a parts detector by regularly taking time to check in with parts, seeing if they have an agenda or are disturbed in any way.

- Talk with a trusted adult who will help you have compassion for the story that has created your parts. Pain or distress can be eased and, with support, transformed by looking at the event or circumstances.

- Be aware that parts of you may act as protectors and be frightened to look at a part of your history. Always respect the protectors' reason and fear of exploring deeper in the system.
- Develop the quality of innate self-wisdom.
- Learn how to talk for a part, i.e. use the phrase 'a part of me'.

We hope that the following exercises and case studies will help you to see how IFS can be used to understand our internal world.

1. Mapping your parts

We think that this is an important first exercise because it will help you to get to know your internal world. We hope that it will signal the start of a valuable life-practice that will help you integrate your internal family.

Your aim over the next few days will be to get to know some of your parts. If you find yourself getting angry, this will be a part of you. How do you feel about this part? Or, perhaps someone will say something to you and you will feel hurt or sad. A part may start reacting by being critical of the person who has caused you to feel this way. On another occasion, a situation may have triggered a part to be filled with joy and a feeling of elation.

Keep a journal and start creating a map of your parts; use pictures/images that will describe them pictorially, if this helps. Start to be aware about when and in what circumstances the parts are triggered. Remember that all your parts are welcome and have compassion for them.

During a time of silent reflection check in with your parts. See which one(s) are activated in your system. As you sit with them bring healing, loving energy to them; this is your self-energy. At the end of a month review the map of your parts. You may find it useful to share your experience with others.

As you work on your own parts, you will recognise parts behaviour in people close to you. When you notice someone else's parts, then become curious about them, realising that it is just a part of them. Having this understanding will help stop you reacting or commenting inappropriately to a part that needs to express itself. If a child behaves inappropriately then remember to say that you notice a part of the child is doing something. Do not identify the whole of the child as misbehaving, otherwise they might come to believe that this is their identity, e.g. 'I'm a naughty child, so that is the way people see me, so I may as well continue being naughty'.

Next become aware of parts that are acting as managers in your system. Are they protecting an exile? Do you find in some situations you have a dominant voice that seems to be in control? For instance, your partner/boss/colleague starts to criticise something you have done or said. You hear yourself defending your behaviour in an authoritarian, firm voice. Perhaps this part is activated to protect a very young part of you, that has been exiled, that was shamed by an adult when you were a child? You learned this strategy to keep you feeling safe and in control. If a manager thinks that they are losing control of the system then a firefighter may be activated, which may be in the form of drinking excessive alcohol, over-exercising, beginning an extra-marital relationship, or any activity that you might recognise that is trying to stop an extreme emotional response being felt. Such firefighter behaviours appear to give parts temporary respite from their pain.

We hope that you will have some fun mapping your parts and learning to understand those of others. We have found that this process has helped us to have compassion for others and ourselves, thereby creating greater harmony. Also, that our sense of self and its healing energy is much more evident in our lives, which has helped our relationships with others.

2. Mapping parts: pupils

With young children, under the age of seven, we think it is important for the adults around them to use the language of parts without going into the description and role of managers and exiles. For instance, use language such as: 'Connor, that's a part of you that is behaving in that way'.

For young children, help them to understand that they have emotions, thus normalising them. Many classrooms that we visit ask children to indicate on a chart what emotion they are feeling that day. However, we rarely see children being given the opportunity to talk about why they are feeling the way they do. Talk with them about the times when they may feel various emotions such as anger, fear and sadness. Think creatively about lessons you can provide that will help them to understand their internal world.

With children whom you consider are being challenged emotionally then provide a mentoring/nurture session for them, when they can share their experiences within a safe relationship. Some young children may prefer to talk about their feelings in a play therapy session, when they can speak through the voices of plastic animals that are placed in a sand tray. Sometimes young children will prefer to draw and then talk about their feelings.

We think that generally pupils over the age of seven will begin to grasp the IFS concepts. Get them to write about their own story when they are feeling sad, angry or upset, then ask them to write their own story when they are feeling relaxed, happy and full of joy. As we recommend below show aspects of the film *Inside Out* that will help them to grasp the nature of our internal world through the experiences of the main character Riley. We think the film is also excellent curriculum material for secondary school aged pupils.

In secondary schools we would recommend that all pupils be given the knowledge and understanding of the Internal Family System and other useful psychological information, in the context of an Inner Curriculum. What we recommend for adults we also recommend for most children over the age of 11. We recognise that this recommendation has implications for initial teacher training and continual professional development of teachers and support staff. There is no doubt in our minds that such an investment of time and resources would have enormous benefit to individuals and society in general.

3. Neil's teacher Mr Smith

We would like to share a story with you based on one of Neil's own life experiences. As you read it we invite you to consider what he may have experienced in terms of his internal world.

Neil was in his headteacher's office at West Kidlington School, when John Heppenstall, one of the school's exceptionally talented senior teachers, came in and enthusiastically announced: 'Hey Neil, I have so much respect for you. I think the parents' newsletter you wrote this week is fantastic and so brilliantly crafted.'

Neil heard himself replying, 'Come off it John, you're exaggerating. I'm not a very good writer – I just do my best.'

Exasperatedly, John said, 'Neil, it's really great. Who says you can't write?' Neil looked at John sheepishly and replied, 'Don't you know that Mr Smith said that I couldn't write?'

John look bemused and said, 'Who the heck is Mr Smith?'

So Neil explained to John about what had happened when he was a pupil in Mr Smith's class: 'I was a seven-year-old in Mr Smith's class at Lethbridge School, Swindon. I particularly recall a lesson at the beginning of the autumn term when Mr Smith, the class's new teacher, asked us to write about our summer holidays. The lesson routine was to write, draw an illustrative picture and then take it to the teacher's desk to be marked.

'I had just returned from a holiday near Bournemouth, where we had stayed in a caravan with my parents and older brother, Maurice, so I had plenty to write about. I'd had a great time playing in the sea and building sandcastles and could visualise the happy scene clearly in my mind. Industriously, I wrote the required half page with a picture of my brother and me playing in the sea, which I drew in the plain paper space at the top.

'I glowed with the memories of my holiday and felt happy as I took my work to join the queue of children waiting in front of Mr Smith's desk. I wanted Mr Smith to see my work, because I thought he would be pleased with the way that it had been written.

'Eventually I reached the Dickensian figure of Mr Smith, whom I clearly remember with his half-rimmed classes, over which he peered at the children. He took my work in his bony hands. There followed a long expectant pause: he kept looking at the work, staring at me and shaking his head disapprovingly and audibly tutting. With each of his gestures, my heart sank further, as this process seemed interminable. Then, in a somewhat snarling, sarcastic voice, and through clenched teeth, he pronounced loudly enough for the whole class to hear:

'Neil! Do you know, you can't write? You are just like your brother, Maurice, who used to be in my class. He couldn't write either! No capital letters, no full stops, awful spelling – this is dreadful. You just can't write and probably will never be any good as a writer. Do you know, you are a very stupid, pathetic, ignorant little boy.'

'He clipped me on the back of my head and raged, 'Go back to your desk and do it again and stop wasting my time, you imbecile'. I returned to my desk, humiliated, dejected, tears flooding down my face, shamed in front of the class, believing that I was a poor writer and a stupid person. I felt hurt, put down and believed in my inadequacy, and these powerful thoughts and feelings took their root in my emerging sense of self.

'Do you now understand John why I have this sense that I can't write?'

John and Neil talked about the importance of never creating similar experiences for pupils at West Kidlington.

May we invite you to pause and think about what may have happened in Neil's internal world?

Our commentary

We are aware that Mr Smith affected Neil's confidence and the part of him that was shamed has carried a belief about his ability as a writer. Jane has helped to bring the compassion of Neil's self-energy to this part, which has helped the healing process. The part has now transformed into the part of him that gets so much enjoyment when writing.

We hope that the story of Mr Smith will help you and your colleagues understand why some pupils may be carrying beliefs about themselves that may be limiting their potential. Perhaps you can similarly recall an event or circumstance in your own life that may have affected you?

A Year 1 teacher told the next account to us about how a schooling system can trigger parts.

4. I'm not any good!

Sally, a Year 1 teacher, told us about Jack, a summer born boy in her class who lives on a farm. He loves to help his dad and is very knowledgeable about the working of the farm. When Jack first started at school he was full of life, somewhat mischievous, always quick with a smile and always ready to join in with class and group activities. He presented himself as an able boy with lots of practical good sense. He told both his teacher and the children in his class many interesting aspects of both farming and nature.

However, one afternoon he was reading to a volunteer parent, and as Sally passed him he turned to her and said, ' I'm no good because I can't read'.

Sally was genuinely shocked to hear Jack say this, as he seemed to negate his great skill in talking to the class and all his knowledge of nature. She reassured him of his capabilities and potential, but she was left wondering about the relevance of a curriculum that forced young children to 'learn' aspects of the curriculum before they are ready.

Our commentary

Take a moment, pause and invite your own parts to relax before you consider the following points, so that you will connect to your innate self-energy and wisdom.

Now, we invite you to reflect on what might have been going on in Jack's internal world?

Why do you think a part of him equated his not being able to read yet with him not being any good?

In what ways might aspects of the curriculum be harmful to any child's sense of self? How can we alleviate this?

What do you think that teachers, support staff and parents can do to support each child's sense of self on their learning journey?

5. In the toilet

Jane was in a department store toilet in Bristol, UK, when, in the next cubicle, she overheard a person remonstrating with a young child.

'Get back on the toilet! I told you not to get off the toilet, you are so stupid, you don't listen... now just stand there and wait!'

Jane heard nothing from the child, but sensed the child was distressed and didn't know how to respond to the angry part of the adult she was with.

From an IFS perspective what do you think was happening in the internal world of the child? What was happening to the child's parts?

Our commentary

Firstly, the child was sensing the anger part of her parent as she was being shamed. Secondly, her part's understanding that the whole of her is stupid was being reinforced. She wasn't being treated with unconditional positive regard so a part of her might have been taking on this idea of being stupid, because if her Mum says so then it must be true. If this self-limiting idea of being stupid is continually reinforced by the parent then a manager may exile this part. She may even have a firefighter who will distract her when she feels shame.

6. *Inside Out*

We think that the Disney/Pixar film *Inside Out* is an excellent one to use as an introduction to children aged over seven about the emotions in our internal world and the roles that they play.

As they think about Riley's internal world and those of her parents they can begin to see that we all have various parts that influence our thinking and behaviour. It encourages them to accurately name the emotions that they feel and see the role that our emotions play. For instance Joy learns to understand the importance that Sadness plays in Riley's life and that it is always important for us to acknowledge an emotion such as sadness. We have noticed that sometimes parents and others will misname a child's emotions; for instance, often when a child is angry or sad they will be told that they are tired.

7. Create a picture of a part

Following on from the previous exercise, this is a great exercise for primary school aged children. Ask them to think of a part of them, perhaps a part that is happy, angry, sad, disgusted or fearful. Now invite them to create a picture showing how this part feels. We have seen some wonderful examples where children have expressed their emotions pictorially using paints, crayons or felt tips; we're sure you can think of other creative ideas too. Now invite the children to talk with each other about their pictures and what they represent. This is a cathartic exercise that can help children to bring self-energy to their emotional parts.

Our goal through the Inner Curriculum is to support children and adults to resolve issues as they happen and not to store up distress internally. The adults and children use their healing self-energy to come alongside their internal worlds. Children have intuition and as they listen to adults hear things that they do not understand. In such circumstances they may inaccurately fill in the gaps of their knowledge. Someone needs to help them to understand and mediate their understanding; otherwise their system creates a false story that is believed to be the reality. A helpful idea is to have a parts' journal in which children can creatively express their parts. Sometimes writing a letter that they don't intend to send can be another cathartic experience that helps them understand their internal system.

Children from war zones need to be able to tell their story, as do children having suffered from abuse. If their story remains unheard and unresolved then their system remains distressed. Such children need the specialist help of trained counselors and psychotherapists.

8. Teach about the 8 C's of Self-Leadership

As we learn about our parts we realise that they are just parts of us and not our authentic self. Dick Schwartz, founder of IFS, noticed that when the authentic self is in control it could be described as having eight qualities that all begin with the letter c. The aim in this exercise is to help pupils to look at these qualities of self-energy so that they will be able to identify with them when they are experienced. In VbE we recognise these qualities as some of our values, which become our virtues as we live them.

Ask your pupils to think about the meaning of these words and how they can make more use of them in their life, at school and at home. You may think of a creative way to display these values in your classroom so that they can be referenced when pupils are showing them.

- Calm: innate sense of inner peace, the 'I' in the storm.
- Curiosity: non-judgemental inquisitiveness, the beginner's mind.
- Confidence: the ability to face the rollercoaster of life with a sense of being ok.
- Courage: the quality to face up to life's challenges and respond altruistically.
- Clarity: enables us to see truly what is happening, unbiased by assumptions and prejudices.
- Creativity: create space to access our intuition, which gives energy to our capacity for creativity, allowing wisdom to emerge.
- Compassion: capacity to have empathy and witnesses unconditionally the pain of another, whilst remaining openhearted.
- Connectedness: realising that we are not totally separate beings but that we are all connected by our humanity and consciousness to others, nature and the world.

9. Values mentoring

Recently, we joined a skilled teacher in a London school who was working with a group of eight pupils that the school thought would benefit from values mentoring. The session invited the pupils to talk about the values that they liked the most. Each child shared their value and we were impressed with the confidence and enthusiasm that was shown. The teacher skillfully guided the children to consider how knowing about the values affected their behaviour? The teacher did not moralise and sensitively endorsed the children's thinking. We were told that prior to the formation of the group that these pupils had displayed a range of anti-social behaviours. The impact of the group was clear to see and the teacher confirmed that, by talking about real situations that were in the experience of the children, they had made incredible progress in managing their own behaviour.

The teacher was not designated as a special needs support teacher but was a class teacher who was given timetabled opportunities to work with these children. It demonstrated to us that the role of the teacher is in the process of changing, from being one that primarily creates opportunities for learning and acquiring knowledge to one that also supports children therapeutically.

Why is it important to help children therapeutically, through a process we describe as values mentoring? One of the main reasons is that values mentoring can create a safe space and time to think about our thoughts, emotions and behaviours that affect our level of wellbeing. Also to give the opportunity to name events in our lives that may be painful for us to think about. By consciously thinking about and naming them in the context of a secure mentor-pupil relationship we have the opportunity to place them into a coherent narrative – the story we tell about ourselves. This process helps us to reintegrate painful parts of our story from which we have dissociated. The result is that by naming the source of the pain we decrease shame and promote healing.

We invite you to think about the five P's from IFS, which are given as a guide for therapists to reflect on when working with their clients.

The five P's are:

- Present: non-judgemental deep listening. Keep your voice calm and voice steady. Be aware of your own parts responses, acknowledging them quietly internally, so that you remain truly present in self-energy.
- Persistence: judging when to maintain focus on the story or to give the child time to pause and an opportunity to re-visit this later.
- Patience: trust that the system knows best the pace of its healing. Remember to respect the role of all protectors in the system.

- Perspective: remember parts are often very young children, there's no need to be scared. Maintain your own self-energy.

- Playfulness: remembering that parts are invariably young, they will enjoy a playful approach.

This brings us to the end of our Inner Curriculum chapter that has focused on the therapeutic process known as IFS – the Internal Family System. We hope that it has inspired you to work with its understanding of our internal world. The next section will look more generally at activities drawn from a range of sources that will further support both your own development and that of your pupils.

Chapter 6:
Useful organisations and activities

'A year from now you may wish you had started today.'

– Karen Lamb

In this chapter we suggest a number of organisations and a range of activities that we think will support you as you construct your Inner Curriculum. We do not want to be prescriptive about what materials you should use, as we are aware that there are so many brilliant resources that we have not referenced that may support you. We have generally referenced organisations in the UK, but we are aware that if you live in another country you should be able to find similar ones nearer to you. We invite you to become an Inner Curriculum detective, sourcing activities and resources that are relevant for the particular pupils that you teach or support.

1. Myers Briggs Personality Type Indicator (MBTI)

In adult team building it is very useful to be aware of the different personality types that make up the team. Does a leader look to bring in members to the team who have similar personalities or those who will compliment the team because they have a different type of personality. The Myers Briggs Personality Type Indicator uses the theory of psychological types, based on much of Carl Jung's thinking, and gives great insight in to differences in personalities, and the positive attributes of each type. For a further insight into this personality indicator visit on the web the Myers and Briggs Foundation, which you will find at www. myersbriggs.org. We think that the indicator is both insightful and fun to use. It will give you further clarity about your own internal world and those of your colleagues.

2. Activities taken from Transactional Analysis.

Eric Berne's Transactional Analysis is another excellent therapeutic discipline that we highly commend to you. Jane studied Eric's relational therapeutic theory, gaining her MSc in its practice as a TA psychotherapist, prior to continuing her studies in The Internal Family System.

Many schools currently use the theory and practice and you can find out more details about training opportunities by visiting the website www.educational-ta.net or by contacting Jane through www. valuesbasededucation.com.

We are aware that we are giving a simple introduction to TA, which we hope will inspire you to look into the concepts at greater depth. Here are some of the key concepts that will support you:

1.   **'I'm ok and you're ok'**

     All relationships should be based on the idea that 'I'm ok and you're ok'. If you sense that a significant relationship at home or at work is not in this 'ok' zone then we suggest you reflect on what prevents you achieving this with the other person(s). As you reflect, maybe you will begin to see steps you can take, which will ultimately support a relationship based on 'I'm ok and you're ok'.

2.   **Strokes**

     In education, this concept focuses on the importance of giving others positive feedback, which are called 'strokes'. We are aware that strokes can be negative. Start by giving yourself strokes because we need to have a good relationship with ourselves. Ensure that stokes you give others are authentic. Consider whether you maybe taking someone for granted. Have you recently given that person some strokes? Are there some 'hidden' people in your life that would benefit from receiving strokes from you – the quiet pupils in your class who can be relied upon to get on with their work and who don't demand your attention, for example? Some children, because of their life experiences, will find it difficult to hear praise in the form of positive strokes. Remember it is important to build up a nurturing relationship with children, using appropriate language that they will understand.

3. **Collecting stamps**

    In our relationships we have experiences, which leave us with feelings, such as resentment, and at the time we do not say anything to the person about our feeling of being hurt. Each time we have one of these experiences it is called a stamp – a little like collecting supermarket stamps except that they have a negative value. However, when we have collected a lot of stamps from the same person we can feel overwhelmed and then erupt, cashing in the stamps all at once. This means we tell the person how upset we are and list all the times that they have upset us. The learning here is that we should always conduct our relationships aiming for open, honest communication that stops the collection of stamps. Can you think of a time that you have collected stamps and then cashed them in, probably inappropriately?

4. **Ego States**

    TA teaches that we have three ego states from which we transact our relationships. One is the Parent ego state. When we are in this state we will sound like a parent, which can be controlling or nurturing, or someone in command. Do you ever catch yourself sounding like your mother or father? Another is the Child ego state. If you are talking or acting as though you are a child, you are in this ego state. The last ego state, the most important one, is called the Adult. In this ego state you are your authentic self and responding to situations in the moment with awareness, spontaneity and intimacy and open, honest communication from the heart. We should aim to conduct our relationships from this Adult ego state. Teachers can transact with pupils from their Parent ego state to the pupil's Child ego state. A VbE classroom aims to transact its teaching/relationships from all the positive aspects of the ego states; ideally from Adult to Adult ego states – yes a child has an Adult ego state! Have some fun by being aware about your ego states and also observe others and think about the ego state that they may be using.

3. Philosophy for Children – P4C

We have observed P4C being used in schools and think that it is an excellent way to enable pupils to consider issues philosophically. The enquiry-based process develops their thinking, curiosity and ability to use language to talk about dilemmas and issues that do not have simple answers. For instance, existential or moral questions such as: why do we exist, why do we have wars and why are so many people starving in our world? A values-based classroom fosters the development of deep listening and having time to reflect on your thinking. P4C is a wonderful way of giving structured opportunities for this to happen. You will find more information at www.philososphy4children.co.uk.

4. The Nurture Group Network

According to their website www.nurturegroups.org: 'The concept of nurture highlights the importance of social environments – who you're with, and not who you're born to – and its significant influence on behaviour and cognitive ability. Children and young people who have a good start in life have a whole host of advantages over those who don't have such positive experiences at home when they are little. They tend to do better at school, attend regularly, enjoy activities with friends and are significantly less likely to offend or experience problems with poor physical or mental health. Nurture groups offer an opportunity to learn the early nurturing experiences some children and young people lack, giving them the skills to do well at school, make friends and deal more confidently and calmly with the trials and tribulations of life, for life.

'Nurture groups are founded on evidence-based practices and offer a short-term, inclusive, focused intervention that works in the long term. Nurture groups are classes of between 6 and 12 children or young people in early years, primary or secondary school settings, supported by the whole staff group and parents. Each group is run by two members of staff. Children attend nurture groups but remain an active part of their main class group, spend appropriate times within the nurture group according to their need and typically return full time to their own class within two to four terms. Nurture groups assess learning and social and emotional needs and give whatever help is needed to remove the barriers to learning. There is great emphasis on language development and communication. Nothing is taken for granted and everything is explained, supported by role modelling, demonstration and the use of gesture as appropriate. The relationship between the two staff, always nurturing and supportive, provides a role model that children observe and begin to copy. Food is shared at 'breakfast' or 'snack time' with much opportunity for social learning, helping children to attend to the needs of others, with time to listen and be listened to. As the children learn academically and socially they develop confidence, become responsive to others, learn self-respect and take pride in behaving well and in achieving.'

We have witnessed the excellent work of the Nurture Group Network and recommend them to you.

5. *Relax Kids*

We highly recommend the *Relax Kids* audios, videos, booklets and resources, particularly for children aged seven and under. It's a great resource for schools and parents to help their children to learn how to relax and also to focus their attention. Simple and very entertaining visualisations/commentaries are used to help the child to access their internal world. Have a look at www.relaxkids.com for ways to access the materials.

6. Mindfulness in schools project

You may have heard of the Mindfulness in schools project known as mindfulnessinschools.org/what-is-b/b-curriculum/. It is popularly known as '.b', which is pronounced [dot-be]. It is the UK's leading mindfulness curriculum for 11 to 18-year-olds in schools. The .b stands for 'stop and be', a simple practice at the heart of this ten-lesson course. Each .b lesson (between 40 minutes and an hour) is expertly crafted for use in the classroom to teach a distinct mindfulness skill. The .b materials are designed to engage even the most sceptical of young minds.

We recommend .b to you.

7. Emotion coaching

Emotion Coaching, www.emotioncoachinguk.com, uses moments of heightened emotion and resulting behaviour to guide and teach the child or young person about more effective responses. Through empathetic engagement, the child's emotional state is verbally acknowledged and validated, promoting a sense of security and feeling 'felt'. This activates changes in the child's neurological system, which allows the child to calm down, physiologically and psychologically.

You will find lots of help and support on their website including training opportunities.

8. Drama and play therapies

During our visits to schools we have seen both drama and play being used as effective therapies to help children access their internal worlds.

For information about these creative methods we recommend, as a first step you can look at the websites of The British Association of Dramatherapists (BADth) www.badth.org.uk .You will discover that Dramatherapy has, as its main focus, the intentional use of healing aspects of drama and theatre as the therapeutic process. It is a method of working and playing that uses action methods to facilitate creativity, imagination, learning, insight and growth.

For Playtherapy look at www.playtherapy.org.uk, which is the UK Society for Play and Creative Arts Therapies (PTUK). The site is intended to provide a complete information resource for therapeutic play, play therapy, filial play and creative arts therapies. It's designed for anyone interested in helping children with emotional literacy, behaviour or mental health problems.

9. Twenty-six great ideas to help primary and secondary school aged pupils access the Inner Curriculum:

1.   **Hot Seating**. A child sits on a chair in the middle or front of the class. Members of the class share with the child the qualities they like and witness in him/her.

     A variation of this, but less intimidating for some pupils, is to give each child a piece of card that they pin or tape to their backs. They are then invited to walk round and class members write their qualities on the card. They then sit down and read out the qualities that have been recognised in them. This exercise often helps children who are reluctant to acknowledge the qualities that they have.

2.   **Guess who?** In this activity a member of the class describes someone's qualities without naming them. Others guess who it is?

3.   **Visualisation: the journey to the clearing in the wood.** The adult describes to the class or the group a journey across a field to a wood where there is a clearing. The journey is described in some detail as each person visualises himself or herself being on the journey.

     On arriving in the clearing a wise person is met who has a gift for you contained in a beautiful box. The lid of the box is opened; you discover three coloured precious stones on which are written three qualities that will help you in your journey of life. You give thanks to the kind person who gave you the gift and retrace your steps through the wood and field to where you started. As you return you feel very happy and content that you have these three wonderful gifts.

Following the visualisation you can invite children to share with each other what gifts they were given. Some may like to share with the class.

With all inner work, may we remind you of our health warning? Neil once conducted this exercise with a group of students at a training college for teachers. One came up to him afterwards to say that the person in the clearing who had given her the gifts was her recently deceased grandmother. The student was not unduly upset, but it alerted him to always give the option of the 'opt-out' if a visualisation is likely to cause any upset.

4. **Russian doll exercise.** Share with the group that a Russian doll has many layers, as in a sense we do too. On the outside we have our physical appearance, and we may appear to have certain characteristics. However, when we begin to peel away the various layers of ourselves, built up during our life, we find a beautiful jewel at the centre. In our Russian doll we put a plastic gem that looks like a large diamond.

   This exercise is one that we recommend if you are helping pupils or others to understand The Internal Family System that we described earlier in the guide.

5. **Emotions journal.** Invite pupils to keep a personal journal about their internal world. It gives an opportunity to bring into consciousness the mood we may be in and the reasons why we have been sensing certain emotions. We are sure that you will think of variations on this idea.

6. **An emotions tree.** Have a colourful display that shows a tree. The pupils make the leaves, on which they write an emotion that they are feeling or have felt. They also write a couple of sentences describing the emotion and the situation when they felt it. This exercise leads to a discussion about emotions and the roles that they play in our lives.

7. **Letterbox.** This is kept in the classroom and pupils are invited to write a note if they want to share how they are feeling and can't directly talk about it with an adult. Such an activity needs very sensitive handling so that pupils do not feel shamed by revealing their innermost thoughts and feelings to you.

8. **Letter to the universe.** In this exercise, the pupil is invited to think about their ambitions (meaning and purpose). They can draw a picture of a young child and older ones can combine writing and drawing. These are then metaphorically beamed into space, to a planet that can be represented by a model in the classroom. They are kept for a period of time in the model planet and then, later in the school year, brought back to Earth for further discussion. For instance, what skills and attributes do I need to achieve my ambition?

9. **The Wisdom Cycle.** Explain to the pupils that they can access a very special personal tool that is called the Wisdom Cycle. They can use it at any time that they feel overwhelmed or are not sure what response to give. The cycle is simple but so very helpful, as it gives us space to think. The cycle is to pause and think before speaking or taking an action.

   If the children are learning about their brain they will see that the cycle helps them not to be overwhelmed by their limbic system that can be quick to respond when they are upset or emotionally highly charged. We have seen children as young as six using the wisdom cycle to great affect.

10. **Lucky dip.** Have a bag in which you have the schools values/ virtues written on pieces of card. Invite pupils to draw out a value and then talk about what this value means to them. How do they use it? Can they describe a time when knowing the value was helpful to them?

11. **Dilemmas.** Great activity for older primary and secondary school aged pupils. The spacecraft! A spacecraft is returning to Earth and on the spacecraft are six people. The captain

announces that the spacecraft only has enough oxygen for five of the people to survive the journey. What do you do? Primary school pupils can also talk with staff about real dilemmas that the school faces. For instance, how to organise break times so that it is a happy and meaningful experience for all.

For older secondary school pupils, a dilemma that we have observed is one about the morality of science helping some women to artificially conceive a child when the world is overpopulated. The teacher whom we observed handled the ensuing debate with a Year 12 group with great skill and sensitivity. She really challenged the group to think deeply about the issues involved.

Another Year 10 group discussed the National Health Service (NHS) and the dilemmas it faces on who should receive treatment. Is there a difference, if funding is scarce, about whether a younger or older person should receive treatment?

12. **Staff ethical dilemmas.** In Estonian schools, staff are invited to consider ethical dilemmas associated with the life and organisation of their schools. At a staff meeting they are presented with a dilemma in the form of a game. Various scenarios are described and staff members are invited to reflect on them. This activity creates a values-based atmosphere in which all voices are equally valued.

13. **Enhancing communicative competence.** We are in no doubt that a well constructed inner curriculum helps in the development of real self-confidence (not arrogance). It is our understanding too that one, if not the most important, of personal skills to be enhanced for life in our complex world is what is termed 'communicative competence'.

As a teacher, Neil has always wanted to give his pupils every opportunity to develop this skill. He did it by encouraging them to take an active part in the teaching process by taking responsibility to teach fellow pupils aspects of the curriculum (under his watchful gaze). This is what he describes as the tutorial method, a process in which he took part in as a doctoral student at Oxford University. We learn best what we have to teach!

Pupils can be given responsibility to talk in school assemblies and to take part in dramatic productions in which they have to speak aloud to large groups. Debating is also a key method for developing communicative competence.

14. **Service learning.** This gives pupils responsibility for identifying real needs in the community and taking practical action. A group of pupils from Poynton High School were taken to Ecuador and the Galapagos Islands for a rich ecological experience and opportunities to engage in projects for local communities, including: teaching in a school and creating a shower and toilet for a local family. The pupils' values were given practical expression as they helped people less privileged than themselves. Many of the pupils reported that the activity had profoundly changed how they see the world as it had expanded their understanding about people in different countries.

Another example of service learning comes from Sandylands Primary School in Morecambe where the pupils found that there was no money in the community to repair the war memorial. They decided to raise funds through various methods including cake sales and the money was raised to the delight of the local Council. These examples show how the internal worlds of pupils can be positively affected if they are given real opportunities to be of service to the community both at home and abroad.

15. **Class thermometer.** This shows the degree to which the class or group is calm and purposeful. Invite the pupils to consider how much of their day they feel calm and purposeful. This should not imply that they should feel a lack of energy, vitality or excitement – all of which can be experienced whilst

remaining calm. The executive function of the brain remains in control, as we learned in the section of the guide that describes the functioning of our brains.

16. **Being a famous film or pop star.** Ask the pupils to think of their favourite star and describe how they see them and why they like them. Now invite the pupils to consider what the star may be like on the inside.

    Are they confident and what values guide their behaviours? What emotions do they think the star has when they are performing in public? Is being a star always a happy role? Older pupils may like to conduct a similar exercise thinking about politicians and world leaders.

17. **Role-play an emotion.** Small groups make up short plays showing someone expressing an emotion. The class has to guess which emotion is being displayed.

18. **Turning the volume up on a value and its internal quality.** In this exercise the pupils think about a value such as peace, trust and honesty; describing what it feels like inside to have these values.

19. **Eye contact exercise.** The pupils sit in pairs and have eye contact with each other. The pupils are either 'a' or 'b'. First, a transmits a feeling they are having to b, and b thinks about what the feeling might be. They then swap roles. Each then shares with the other to see if they had been able to 'read' the other person. This is a good exercise to help pupils to pay attention to the subtleties of body language.

20. **Opposite opinions/polarised thinking.** Secondary school aged pupils will enjoy this exercise. Divide the pupils into two lines 'a' and 'b' facing each other. Decide on a controversial topic, e.g. should we allow refugees in to this country. Pupils in line 'a' represent the point of view against allowing refugees in, even if this is not their point of view. Pupils in line 'b'

represent the opinion that we should let refugees in, even if this is not their opinion. They are then all given a couple of minutes to shout out randomly, as they feel moved to, all the reasons that support the point of view they are representing. Then there is a pause, and all pupils are invited to reflect on how they are feeling.

The second stage of the exercise is to invite each pupil to shout out what they are frightened of if their point of view is ignored. After a couple of minutes there is another pause. The third part of this exercise is for the pupils in both lines to relay what they heard from each other; in particular, what touched them emotionally.

The pupils are then brought together to talk generally about the issue and whether anyone's argument helped change their view about the issue. The object is to help pupils to think widely and deeply about real issues and avoid prejudice or any other social conditioning that stops them looking at an issue with compassion and objectivity.

The concept of encouraging people to talk about what they are frightened of if their point of view is ignored is an important part of conflict resolution. Often, once our fears have been expressed and acknowledged, we become less rigid in our point of view and more open to listen to other views.

21. **Strange emotions!** This is a fun activity as you ask pupils to say something, perhaps a story or joke, but with an unusual emotion. For instance, telling a funny story with a serious voice. This exercise gives an opportunity to accurately name emotions. Many of us confuse our understanding of emotions because they were wrongly labelled when we were young. For instance, 'Oh John, you're behaving like that because you're tired'. John is not really tired, he is actually just angry!

22. **Self-leadership (agency).** This gives pupils the opportunity to take responsibility for leading an activity. They are asked to

be mindful to be guided by their inner qualities (values). They report back about how easy or difficult they found this to do. What stops them being authentic – who they want to be?

23. **Charters and pledges.** Pupils sign up to a school, class or form charter – the way we are going to behave and learn together. The pupils make pledges about what they are going to do as an active member of the school community.

24. **Pass on Bonzo.** Primary school pupils love this activity. The school has a cuddly toy, appropriately named, which is passed from a child when another is spotted living one of the school's values. This activity raises values awareness and makes children aware of the affect on others of their internal world.

25. **The world of the community.** This involves bringing community leaders, local heroes and inspiring role models into school to share with pupils the motivation for doing what they do.

These sessions work best when pupils have had time to research the person and prepare their thinking, which will guide their questions. We watched such a session with a holocaust survivor – a real educative experience for pupils and adults alike.

26. **Holding a family meeting.** Finally, an activity for families to use at home. The two of us find that holding a regular meeting, where we can have the opportunity for blue-sky thinking about what we are doing in our lives, is very important to us. If we don't allocate time for our meeting then time goes on and our diary gets filled with the demands that others place on us. Our meeting also gives us an opportunity to talk about aspects of our lives that may be worrying us, or are causing unnecessary anxiety or stress.

We avoid our meetings becoming a moaning shop. We find that having had these creative sessions, a great deal of what we talk about actually happens. We write down our own priorities in the diary to make sure we have 'us' time. May we commend this for your family – yes, include children if you have them as it gives them the opportunity to contribute and for you to deeply listen to what your child/children want you to hear.

Another related idea for use at home is one we gained from our reading the writings of Thich Nhat Hahn, the Vietnamese peace activist. He suggested the idea of having a breathing space or room in your home. This is somewhere that any member of the family can go voluntarily if they feel angry or distressed in any way. It allows the person to calm down and not fall into the trap of saying things that are later regretted. Many schools think about ways of providing safe spaces for pupils to calm down, which we advocate.

We hope that these ideas and simple exercises have whetted your creative appetite for forming activities that will act as a gateway to a child's internal world. We are convinced that they will support an inner curriculum, through which the pupil has a deeper understanding of their thoughts, feelings, sensations and emotions. These are the foundations that make them who they are and influence the responses they make to the external world.

We wish you well as you explore and use the ideas to create an Inner Curriculum and please, if you need any support contact www. valuesbasededucation.com.

The Future?

'The future lies before you, like paths of pure white snow. Be careful how you tread it, for every step will show.'

– Unknown

We were in Iceland recently where we gave a presentation at a conference entitled, 'The Spirit of Humanity'. People from a variety of backgrounds and disciplines were brought together to consider how we could promote the flourishing of humanity by focusing on what is happening that is positive. Our presentation was given with teachers from Álfaheidi School, a popular Icelandic values-based school for children aged from one to seven.

The highlight of the presentation was a video that showed, in ways that words fail to do, the nurturing power of a school that is founded on positive human values, attachment, empowering relationships and a creative inner curriculum, which gives children a range of meaningful foundation experiences for life. The video, through simple photographs of these young children living their values, touched the hearts of the audience and was met by spontaneous applause when it ended. There was a powerful intuitive understanding that if all children received a similar education then humanity could be transformed.

We believe that young children are close to the soul of humanity and need our support to maintain their inquisitiveness, openness and natural desire to learn and experience. VbE and its inner curriculum focuses on the human spirit, our essence, all that is unseen but is real, such as thoughts and emotions, experiences that create awe and wonder, and the realisation of the connectedness of humanity.

When Neil and his colleagues developed the first explicitly values-based school in Oxfordshire, he knew that there would be people who would think it a distraction from the school's core business, or that such a emphasis should not be the focus for mainstream schools. He also knew that in order to satisfy the misgivings of many, he would have to demonstrate the impact of VbE as a practical philosophy that would effectively combine a knowledge and character-based curriculum.

Professor Terry Lovat from Australia visited the school and wanted the work he witnessed to influence the development of values education in Australia. This he did, with an investment of $40 million in the process. The impact of the initiative was researched and the benefits were firmly established.

In the UK, Neil was invited to conferences to talk about the differences that having values central to a school's life made. The work started to find root in many other school communities and so a quiet revolution began. Neil was convinced that systemic change would be slow, as the national agenda was focused on raising standards through a process of naming and shaming those who didn't meet the criteria laid down for attainment in the basic subjects. Neil was criticised by some education leaders for his grass roots approach rather than being more strategic in convincing politicians and other opinion leaders to support his views.

Neil decided to continue working under the establishment's radar, holding on to the view that real change will happen when enough school communities are values-based and the benefits are clearly seen by parents and the community. It is at this point that the political system will take the work seriously, as they have to take account of the wishes of their constituents. This slow process is now nearing a tipping point as we see that the movement for placing character development at the centre of education is being taken seriously. Most people now appreciate that our future depends on the character traits that are nurtured in families, schools and universities. As the Professor of Ethics at Tartu University in Estonia said to us, an education system should be judged by how young people turn out 30 years later. What sort of people have we produced? What has been their contribution to society? What is our hope for the future?

From our experience, we see that so many people live a life with an existential vacuum, without a meaning and purpose that drives their thinking and cautions their behaviour. Many seem subject to the whims and influence of minds that reinforce the limiting aspects of humanity. We observe that if so many people feel disenfranchised, unheard, unvalued and feel deeply without peace, then political leaders are elected who reflect this internal chaos. An extreme example of this phenomenon was the rise to power of Hitler after the First World War.

Although the foregoing seems pessimistic, we actually remain optimistic because we can see a counter-movement being spawned. This movement is nudging towards a transformation of human consciousness, and is one that is built on the understanding that, although we appear separate from each other, we share the same consciousness. Such an understanding means that we have an equal responsibility to each other. It prevents us from using our limbic responses, such as fear and mistrust, to label others that we don't know as enemies. To survive on a planet with such a vast population we have to cooperate and ensure equity in terms of resources and wealth, otherwise competition for resources leads to war, famine and disease.

Our understanding is that children need to be given a set of life skills that will help them access their internal worlds. This will enable them to be led in their thoughts and actions by what we describe as self-energy, which is the innate healing energy that is at the core of our being. People who profess a religious tradition may call this energy soul or spirit.

We believe that the starting point for education should be based on forming good relationships and understanding how we create them. Early childhood education has recognised the primacy of such work, but those who don't understand or appreciate the stages of child development often want the focus of schooling to be on other things, such as basic writing or reading skills. Of course, neither is mutually exclusive, but we have seen in schools that first promote the development of relational skills that other basic skills follow more naturally when good relationships have been established first. We urge that this pedagogy is continued and developed throughout the stages of education, with secondary school aged pupils being supported to delve deeply into values awareness. For instance, in lessons they will consider how to face and help resolve the ethical dilemmas of the 21st century in preparation for their lives as adults.

We propose that Values-based Education is the first educational methodology in the world that nurtures both the spiritual awakening of people, through practices such as reflection/mindfulness, and the higher orders of consciousness, which take people from a focus on themselves (egocentric), or their group (ethnocentric), to an understanding of the interconnectedness of humanity and the natural world (cosmic-centric). History shows how a lack of understanding about the importance of these two aspects working together has led to people not reaching their human potential, resulting in disharmony, violence and war. In other words, peace does not come about if someone has a spiritual awakening, but if they have not reached the higher orders of consciousness; leaving them locked into an ethnocentric worldview, driven by such thoughts as 'to be saved everyone has to believe what my group believes'. If the same person has a cosmic-centric understanding then they will respect the ideals of others.

In order to release the creative dynamic of human consciousness and take the lid off pupil potential, we encourage parents, school leaders, teachers and support staff to see the importance of schools having a prime focus on the development of wellbeing and resilience through the Inner Curriculum, which we believe is the missing link in education.

Our mission is to support children and young people so that they will become values-led adults and parents of the future, accessing their innate self-energy as they embrace Values-based Living. We are convinced that if each of us learns how to integrate our internal world then the positive impact on the external world will be profound, as humanity will become more integrated and enable us to live in harmony.

We hope we have given you enough information so you are able to enhance the wellbeing and resilience of yourself and others by implementing an Inner Curriculum, which we are confident has the power to enhance individual lives and the sustainability of our wonderful world.

Now, over to you...

Bibliography

Berne, E. (1975): *What Do You Say After You Say Hello?* London: Corgi.

Brown, D. (2010): *Giving Voice to the Impacts of Values Education: The Final Report of the Values in Action Schools Project.* Melbourne: Education Services Australia Ltd.

Cozolino, L. (2013): *The Social Neuroscience of Education: Optimizing Attachment and Learning in the Classroom.* New York: W. W. Norton & Company.

Frankl, V. (1959): *Man's Search For Meaning.* London: Rider.

Fuller, A. (2014): *Tricky Teens: How to create a great relationship with your teenager... without going crazy!* Sydney: Finch Publishing.

Hawkes, N. (2003): *How to Inspire and Develop Positive Values in Your Classroom.* Cambridge: LDA Learning.

Hawkes, N. (2005): *Does teaching values improve the quality of education in primary schools? A Study about the Impact of Introducing Values Education in a Primary School.* Beau-Bassin, Mauritius: VDM Publishing House.

Hawkes, N. (2013): From *My Heart: Transforming Lives Through Values.* Carmarthen: Independent Thinking Press.

Lovat, T, Toomey, R, Dally, K and Clement, N. (2009): *Project to Test and Measure the Impact of Values Education on Student Effects and School Ambience.* University of Newcastle, Australia: Department of Education, Employment and Workplace Relations.

Lucas, S, Insley, K and Buckland, G. (2006): *Nurture Group Principles and Curriculum Guidelines. Helping Children to Achieve.* London: The Nurture Group.

Morgan, N. (2017): *Taught Not Caught: Educating for 21ˢᵗ Century Character.* Melton: John Catt Educational Ltd.

Reay, A. (2017): *The Power of Character: Lessons from the frontline.* Melton: John Catt Educational Ltd.

Schwartz, R. C. (2001): *Introduction to the Internal Family Systems Model.* Illinois: Trailheads, Division of The Centre for Self Leadership.

Siegel D. J. (1999): *The Developing Mind: How Relationships and the Brain Interact to Shape Who We Are: Towards a Neurobiology of Interpersonal Experience.* New York: The Guilford Press.

Woodrow, F. (2017): *Compass For Life.* London: Elliott and Thompson.

About the Authors

Neil Hawkes

Neil is a well-respected global educational leader, thinker and social commentator. Neil's successful career as an educator in the UK started by learning his craft as a teacher, which he loved. Neil is always proud to describe himself as a teacher. Three headships, and senior educational leadership positions in county education authorities followed. Whilst he was a county chief adviser for education, he decided to return to a school headship in Oxfordshire to implement his transformational ideas, which promote wellbeing, resilience and self-leadership.

Neil spent seven years as Headteacher of West Kidlington School where the school gained an international reputation for its transformational curriculum. It was here that the school community worked together to devise and implement a system of education based on learning about and living a community inspired set of values. Consequently, what is now known as Values-based Education (VbE) was born, which is recognised internationally as the foundation of outstanding educational practice.

Neil is well known as an inspirational speaker, broadcaster and writer. His previous book, *From My Heart: Transforming Lives Through Values*, is a celebration of the success of his work worldwide.

Neil is married to Jane.

Jane Hawkes

Jane is an experienced and highly respected psychotherapist. For many years Jane worked as an innovative trainer and guidance counsellor, supporting disaffected young people. Jane actively supports the theoretical and practical development of Values-based Education (VbE) worldwide and is one of its key thinkers and presenters.

In recent years she has studied the Internal Family System (IFS) of psychotherapy in the UK and USA. Her particular academic and professional interests are focused on supporting both adults and children to understand their inner world of thoughts, sensations, emotions and behaviours. She believes that as we compassionately open our hearts and minds to our internal world, it releases our sense of self, which is essential when establishing a peaceful, loving world.